Praise for **LOWEST WHITE BOY**

"Greg Bottoms is one of the most innovative and intriguing nonfiction writers at work, and this is his most powerful book to date, a crucial interrogation of whiteness, white supremacy, and the formation of one American lowest white boy."

—Jeff Sharlet, author of
The Family: The Secret Fundamentalism at the Heart of American Power

"Greg Bottoms takes readers on a journey through ignorance and enlightenment in this dazzling memoir about growing up white and working class in the slowly desegregating South. He treats his subjects with compassion as he explores the tangle of race relations in his childhood. *Lowest White Boy* should be read alongside *Citizen: An American Lyric* by Claudia Rankine, in that everyday experiences of racism are illuminated with rich and powerful meaning. A consummate storyteller, Bottoms brings to life a world that is rarely explored in contemporary conversations about racial strife. The result is a narrative that is as beautiful as it is instructive."

—Emily Bernard, author of *Black Is the Body: Stories from My Grandmother's Time, My Mother's Time, and Mine*

"I read *Lowest White Boy* with serious admiration. It's difficult to think of a timelier, nervier, more discomfiting, more pulse-quickening book than Greg Bottoms's impressive exploration of an extremely difficult subject. There is candor and then there is candor. This is candor."

—David Shields, author of
Black Planet: Facing Race during an NBA Season

"From the first page on, I was totally absorbed in this 'memoir as vehicle for interpretation,' as Greg Bottoms describes *Lowest White Boy*. It's a passionate hybrid text that moves seamlessly between the personal and the public, the timely and the timeless. Raised in Tidewater, Virginia, 'at ground zero of American slavery,' Bottoms imagined as a young boy feeling the 'layers of time beneath [his] feet.' A gifted storyteller, he evokes this feeling in each of the poignant, troubling vignettes he offers his lucky readers."

—Rebecca McClanahan, author of
*The Tribal Knot: A Memoir of Family, Community,
and a Century of Change*

LOWEST WHITE BOY

IN PLACE
Jeremy Jones, Series Editor
Elena Passarello, Series Editor

Far Flung: Improvisations on National Parks, Driving to Russia, Not Marrying a Ranger, the Language of Heartbreak, and Other Natural Disasters
Cassandra Kircher

On Homesickness: A Plea
Jesse Donaldson

Lowest White Boy   Greg Bottoms

WEST VIRGINIA UNIVERSITY PRESS · MORGANTOWN 2019

ISBN:

Paper 978-1-946684-96-7

Ebook 978-1-946684-97-4

Library of Congress Cataloging-in-Publication Data

Names: Bottoms, Greg, author.

Title: Lowest white boy / Greg Bottoms.

Description: Morgantown, WV : West Virginia University Press, 2019 | Series: In place series

Identifiers: LCCN 2018040446 | ISBN 9781946684967 (pbk.)

Subjects: LCSH: Bottoms, Greg. | Boys–Virginia–Hampton–Biography. | Hampton
       (Va.)–Race relations–History–20th century. | Whites–Race identity–Virginia–
       History–20th century. | African American schoolboys–Virginia–Hampton–Social
       conditions–20th century. | School integration–Virginia–Hampton–Anecdotes. |
       Racism–Virginia–History–20th century–Anecdotes. | Working class–Virginia–
       Tidewater Region–Attitudes–History–20th century. | Anti-racism–Anecdotes. |
       Hampton (Va.)–Biography.

Classification: LCC F234.H23 B67 2019 | DDC 305.8009755412/0904–dc23

LC record available at https://lccn.loc.gov/2018040446

Book and cover design by Than Saffel / WVU Press

Cover image: Anti-busing rally, August 26, 1970. Photograph by Don Pennell, P.71.37.04.

       Reproduced by permission of the Valentine.

[WHITENESS] APPEARS AS SOCIAL, not biological, a powerful social construct letting whites think of themselves first and foremost as individuals. Although white people may exempt themselves from race, white privilege comes into view as a crucial facet of white race identity. At the same time, many other characteristics—class, region, gender, age, able-bodiedness, and sexual orientation—all affect the manifestations of this privilege.

—Nell Irvin Painter, *The History of White People*

FIRST, SOME HISTORICAL and cultural context.

I was born in Hampton, Virginia, in 1970. My family—both sides, mother's and father's—had migrated there, with thousands of others, from eastern North Carolina (Ahoskie, Windsor, and other parts of Bertie County, one of the poorest places in the state, and all along the western shores of the Chowan River) to Tidewater, or Hampton Roads, as it is interchangeably known, in southeastern Virginia in the early part of the twentieth century. They sought a better, more comfortable life and employment opportunities in and around what would later be referred to, by President Eisenhower, as the military industrial complex. We are Scotch-Irish and English, with surnames like Bottoms, Cowan, Lowe, and Carmines and a supposed North American arrival date of 1755 (departing Liverpool?), but with plenty unknown about our background. An aspect of American origins and identities is that they are sometimes only partially built on an edifice of sturdy facts or reasonable and nonexpedient interpretations. The world, in human terms, becomes the set of stories you believe about the world.

I awoke into consciousness—into cognition and retrievable memory-making—as a child during the time of busing and school integration in the mid- to late 1970s, and my mother, for some of that time, was a public school bus driver. She was one of only several Southern white people whom I had never heard say something negative about a person solely because of the color of their skin. Like many women at that time and from the white working class, she finished high school and assumed she would be a secretary, or, possibly, if she was willing to do a bit more schooling, a nurse or a teacher. She was intuitively smart and had a huge emotional intelligence and compassion, particularly toward children. She took me with her on the bus most days when I was a little boy. I had a firsthand view of one of the outcomes of civil rights in action without understanding any of it.

From the ages of five to ten, the time of the memory-based stories I present in what follows, I, of course, knew nothing of Southern race relations, or of how we arrived at the tense, binary racial situation I inhabited, or why. I was a product of history, as we all are.

The grim absurdity and devastation of American racism, the underlying white supremacist history and values and beliefs and actions and laws in the South and beyond, have been held in place by fantasies and by fear. "Racism is taught in our society," popular writer Alex Haley famously wrote, "it is not automatic. It is learned behavior toward persons with dissimilar physical characteristics." To paraphrase Barack Obama paraphrasing Nelson Mandela, children are not born racist. Yet an Australian ethnographer and cultural studies scholar presented me with a question not long ago that strikes me as almost a Zen koan: Why is organic *non*-racism so hard to find in the world?

In my American world, as the epigraph opening this book from historian Nell Irvin Painter suggests, white people, even economically insecure and working-class white people without clear and easy access to power, have benefitted from racism—that is just a large-scale systematic and historical fact in regard to housing, schooling, employment, structures of wealth acquisition, and our legal system. I also think it has been damaging in some deep ways, just as holding onto a set of lies and illusions over time can bring about spiritual suffering and mental illness, setting forth, to borrow a phrase from Antonio Gramsci, "a great variety of morbid symptoms." I believe pursuing truth is, or should be, a kind of North Star of human progress, and to ensconce yourself, partially or completely, in delusion, or pettiness, or meanness, or cruelty, or indecency, or unethical or immoral behavior, is a sure way to make yourself lost and sick, and of course the same holds true on the larger scales of communities, regions, and countries.

It is statistically true that most Americans—across races and ethnicities—don't know that after the Civil War, after the Civil Rights Acts of 1866 (citizenship rights) and 1875 (equal treatment in regard to "public accommodations"), after the Thirteenth Amendment (against "slavery and involuntary servitude") and Fourteenth Amendment (equal protection under the law) and Fifteenth Amendment (voting rights) to the United States Constitution, the hope during Reconstruction of promised equal rights for black citizens—former slaves and their offspring—was shown to be empty words and toothless laws only. In 1896, in *Plessy v. Ferguson*, the United States legalized "separate but equal" facilities and services, which was separate and obviously catastrophically unequal, legally stripping African Americans of many rights and cementing the social and cultural condition of privilege and institutionalized racial supremacy for one group and racial subjugation for another, which I only began to learn about, in any specific historical sense, in my early twenties by reading W. E. B. Du Bois's 1903 book *The Souls of Black Folk*, a work given to me in college, where I studied English literature and journalism, by a white travel writer, memoirist, and literary journalist. That book shook me ethically, morally, and spiritually. One aspect of my privilege was that I didn't need to know my country and region's history because it had never been weaponized against me; it had, in fact, been weaponized to protect me.

The United States was built by people of many different backgrounds. The land was colonized beginning in the early seventeenth century and then conceptualized in the late seventeen hundreds as a nation by white, male Europeans on Enlightenment notions of freedom and liberty, of Christian morality, of cleansing through punishment, and of redemption as both possible and sought. Most Americans quickly condemn, as we should, crimes against humanity in other parts of the world (Germany, Italy, Russia, South Africa, Uganda, Bosnia, Rwanda, Sudan, Syria, etc.). Yet it is hard, even now, to fully acknowledge our nation-state's own deeds. (The state of Texas—only one example of "white washing" as common practice—doctored its required high school history textbooks, in 2015, to suggest that slaves were "workers" remembered fondly by land owners for their songs and folk tales.)

America as a nation, for some time, has been able to say, at least speak the words, that race is a wound in the American psyche. We can acknowledge that. Even conservative whites in the South—and I know many—can accept Frederick Douglass's and John Brown's idea that slavery is America's "original sin." The trouble is with directness, clarity. Some words are like harshly revealing mirrors held too close to the face. For instance, we relegate to a distant, detached past that the white Supreme Court of the United States, in the *Dred Scott* ruling of March 6, 1857, written by Justice Taney, regarded black people as an inferior and subordinate class of beings; or that black people were inspected for purchase like farm animals; or that black people were regarded as three-fifths of a human and two-fifths of a beast; or that for centuries a white man killing a black man registered, among most otherwise law-abiding whites, as the moral equivalent of killing a horse or a good farm dog; or that black women and babies were used, regularly, as money and credit in exchanges among whites (including our country's leaders); or that hanging a black person in the first half of the twentieth century (reliable statistics on U.S. lynchings exceed four thousand) was an event not so different in kind and practice than people now gathering around a big-screen TV to cheer on someone pummeling someone else in the Ultimate Fighting Championships on pay-per-view. I remember reading a notice in the pre–Civil War archives of a Richmond, Virginia, paper for a missing slave who could be identified by the thick scar tissue around his wrists and ankles from shackles.

The above, along with contemporary realities like de facto educational segregation, unequal criminal sentencing among black people and white people for the same charges, lopsided statistics on police stops and shootings, and coordinated red state efforts at voter suppression, are unpleasant facts, sickening facts, causational facts haunting present and often passively constructed statistics on poverty, education, wealth, family and community stress and breakdown, incarceration, health, and mortality. White people in America, white people in my South, seem to have perfected complex social psychological methods that deflect our attention from facing our relationship to these facts every second of every day. I think of it sometimes as an impressive magic trick. I'm still trying to figure out and describe how it works.

I went through twelve years of public education at ground zero of American slavery and lived inside its deformed and deforming effects and magical thinking and mystifications and white self-protective propaganda without ever—not once—hearing about civil rights or hearing the phrase "Jim Crow" inside a school building.

If, as a boy in Tidewater, Virginia, I could have sifted through the layers of time beneath my feet, I would have found that on my patch of land, my place, my home, my secular and spiritual site of comfort, *Plessy v. Ferguson*, among a thousand other laws and policies and practices and beliefs and assumptions and attitudes, helped calcify injustice and American apartheid, and then normalized it to such an extent that white boys like me could walk through this world of injustice with smiles on our faces, accepting what had been wrought without pangs of conscience or perhaps even notice.

I didn't know about the Gray Commission, formed by Governor Stanley in 1954 to attempt to insure integration was not enacted in Virginia after the *Brown v. Board* verdict, which led to the Stanley Plan, a white supremacist set of statutes meant to keep African

Americans out of white schools and also curb the legal influence of the Virginia NAACP.

I didn't know about Massive Resistance, the "plan" and all-out assault through the courts on equal rights proposed and promoted by Virginia Senator Harry Byrd.

I didn't know about the power of the KKK in Virginia, especially in the first half of the twentieth century, or about an African American church bombed in Richmond in 1966.

I didn't know about the Southern Manifesto, signed by 101 politicians, mostly Southern Democrats, in 1956, not long before Southern Democrats began moving away from the Democratic Party for the Republican Party because of civil rights and later the nomination of a Northern Catholic named John Kennedy for president.

I didn't know about George Wallace, whose independent platform for president in 1968 was essentially racism against black people, or about Nixon's "Southern Strategy" to cynically divide anxious whites (my family and community) from blacks to gain power and then use that power not to help those working-class whites but to try to cut their social "safety net" programs brought about in the New Deal (a communist idea, according to many newspaper columnists) and further disenfranchise them (the old "poor whites voting against their own interests," which Du Bois pointed out in the 1930s) while deflecting their legitimate resentments back toward nonwhites who were, so the political story went, taking their resources and ruining their country, a meme that, of course, continues to play out to this day and has spawned complex networks of fact twisting, mendacity, epidemic delusion, deeply unethical and powerful media and messaging, and an explicitly and vocally and proudly racist presidency.

I didn't know about the first go-around of the "silent majority" and "America First," the latter made famous before World War II by anti-Semite and fascist sympathizer Charles Lindbergh and which was a reference to protectionism and also an America where white, Christian, male cultural, social, and political power was total and righteous and ordained by God, a version of God, in my view (and I grew up Methodist), twisted into a convenient political shape and projected out of human need and self-referentiality.

This was the context, the backdrop, of my life as a white kid who lived in a little brick house in Hampton, Virginia, and whose mom, who really needed the money, drove a bus full of African American kids from a poor neighborhood to a once all-white school during the time of busing.

It is easier to be blind to the most troubling parts of U.S. history than to understand them. In what follows I am interested in how powerful historical, political, social, and cultural forces are on everyday life, on a young *individual*—me, or at least a remembered version of me from decades ago, for convenient example. George Orwell, in his essay "Why I Write," confesses the contingency of his own work: "In a peaceful age I might have written ornate or merely descriptive books, and might have remained almost unaware of my political loyalties. As it is I have been forced into becoming some sort of pamphleteer." This is not a memoir in a conventional sense. It's memoir as vehicle for interpretation. It's memoir as narrative criticism, as example, as, no doubt, didacticism, even polemic, but I'm feeling impatient these days, like I need to cut to the chase, get to the point.

"Culture is ordinary," wrote Raymond Williams in the late 1950s. Yes. But to a child making new "observations, comparisons, and meanings," culture is as invisible as the air. For decades a white boy in Jim Crow Virginia, in the South, would have been trained, by the ordinariness of culture and the acceptance of this culture, to take for granted that black people were not worthy of going to white schools, or voting, or using toilets or water fountains for whites, or eating in white restaurants. This is the least of it and the list could go on and on.

The white child would have been inculcated to know, for instance, that a black girl would pollute his swimming pool with her skin, or a black boy giving blood to save his life after a bad accident would have poisoned him or perhaps even made it so his mannerisms would become "those of the negro"—the black child's blood a kind of magic potion of inferior and infectious identity (the city of Nashville closed its municipal pools for several years in the early 1960s after two young black men broke with Jim Crow practices and went swimming). This white child would be oblivious on a conscious level and yet know skin color as social brand, as inherent system of American value. Something like white skin equals a quarter; black skin equals a penny. This white child would accept the normal devaluing of other humans, believe it was the way God made us.

Shortly after the episodes that follow, Lee Atwater was chief campaign strategist for Ronald Reagan. He helped orchestrate Reagan's landslide presidential victory over Jimmy Carter. In 1981, he was caught on tape describing the real workings of socially adaptive conservative storytelling and the evolving language of racism. He said, "Y'all don't quote me on this. You start in 1954 by saying 'nigger, nigger, nigger.' By 1968 you can't say 'nigger'—that hurts you. It backfires. So you say stuff like forced busing, states' rights, all that stuff. You're getting so abstract now. You're talking about cutting taxes. And all of these things you're talking about are totally economic things and the by-product of them is blacks get hurt worse than whites." President Lyndon Johnson, Texas Democrat, once said, "If you can convince the lowest white man he's better than the best colored man, he won't notice you're picking his pocket. Hell, give him somebody to look down on, and he'll empty his pockets for you."

I lived among this "lowest white man," was a kind of lowest white boy. I was cloaked every day in cultural and political stories. Things happened behind the scenes. Power was pursued, taken, and shaped.

The country changed. Laws changed. Policy changed. The favored benefitted. The disfavored found more obstacles in the world—but how, from where? Some things I have learned to see and understand. Many things I see and partially understand. And much, of course, is still invisible to me, even as it shapes the reality and the dynamics of power around me. The idea that someone would politically manipulate my community, as Lee Atwater and Lyndon Johnson suggested, to gain power was not something I would have imagined or even fathomed as a child. That my own mind was being formed within a cynically manipulated reality is something painful to acknowledge, even now.

What I am saying is this: the real, insidious power of racism the world over, and in America and the South and my boyhood city in particular, is its ability, in human culture and thought and the nuances of communication, to achieve normalcy in the minds of those benefitting and then take on the character of unquestioned truth.

Family Reunion, 1979

IN 1979, THE YEAR I WAS EIGHT, my father's family reunion was held at a public park in Newport News, Virginia. It was a place of woods and creeks and picnic tables, set against the eastern shore of the southern part of the James River, a few miles before it empties into the Chesapeake Bay. I heard more than one relative that day say they hoped the place wouldn't get *overrun by the locals*, meaning the groups of young black males on bikes or on foot from the surrounding poor neighborhoods. They were often there playing basketball on the cracked and faded courts.

Several of my male cousins and I—four or five white boys— played war in the woods while we waited to be called to the picnic area for lunch, where fifty or so relatives, toddlers to the elderly, would chattily swarm around the splintered tables and pile their flimsy paper plates with fried chicken and salads from KFC and all manner of covered-dish

appetizers and desserts—soft-shell crabs, coleslaw, banana pudding, lemon squares.

After playing for an hour or so in the woods, one of my older cousins, Kevin, a big fourteen-year-old with a mean, crooked-toothed grin and a mom-inflicted haircut, dared me to yell the N-word at the basketball players from behind a thick copse of trees. I was looking out at a full court of ten older black boys and young men, most maybe sixteen to twenty years old, muscles and sweat and back-and-forth joking. One older man—he looked about thirty-five—wore athletic glasses with a band holding them onto his head. I thought he was a teacher, maybe a coach, because everyone listened to him; they waited to see what he would say when there was a foul, a potential foul. He was the center of their disbanding and reforming circles on the court.

I stared at the men and boys, especially at the man I thought was a teacher, and then at the metal hoops and backboards, the falling-down fencing rolled up in places like the edges of once-wet paper. The rims were netless. The backboards looked indestructible, like big, square storm grates, and I had been told, had heard, many times, that that was because blacks (what a strange descriptor, I thought even then, for people with skin of widely varying shades of brown) would steal anything they could carry, even a heavy backboard. When I was very young, because of things white people (who are actually more pink or tan or beige) said, and because I was a child and when you are a child everything said is the truth, there is no such thing as a word that is not the truth—because why would there be?—I imagined the houses of black people were filled with pointless objects, stolen for the sake of stealing. Almost every word out of every mouth that I understood to be trustworthy made me believe that black people operated like rats, running wild in the secret streets, hoarding the unusable.

I'm not going to do that, I said to Kevin, hiding from the court now in the deep-green foliage, sweating in the heat, the wet sunshine, sweating from running and climbing the small hills, hills where Revolutionary War soldiers and Confederate and Union soldiers had walked and climbed and run and screamed and fought and killed and died. We were maybe twenty miles from where Dutch traders dragged and slapped the first African slaves onto American soil in 1619. Sometimes I felt the layers of time beneath my feet—or that is how I remember it, or how it feels now, or something. Smell of honeysuckle. Saw of bees. Penny-colored pine needles. Stripe of gold light stenciled onto green grass. Earth smell so strong it must have come from inside my own head. Virginia. Childhood. I go everywhere in the country, can travel the world, and I sit down to write a sentence and I am still there.

Yeah, you are, said Kevin.

No, I'm not, I said, laughing, trying to make it seem as if the whole thing was ridiculous, would require no more of our attention.

Kevin took out a knife, a little plastic knife from KFC, serrated on one side, translucent and blue tinted, and held it up to my throat as the other cousins stood around watching, though I don't actually remember them doing this, just remember that they were there and that is what they would do in a scene and this is a memoir of sorts, like I said, so I'm kind of remembering and imagining the other cousins, four of them, ragged white boys with filthy clothes and knees and faces or whatever. Dirt-creased necks, black-edged fingernails. I could tap into some working-class white people stereotypes, if those images are useful. Maybe I'll use the phrase "trailer park" as a place holder in this draft.

Do it or I'll cut your throat, Kevin said.

I thought about it, yelling the word and then running and it would all really just be a game, some fun at the reunion, but I didn't want to do it because the man, I still believed, was a teacher of some kind, and he was teaching the boys playing and maybe not only basketball but other things, too, because he kept stopping to talk to them and pat them on the back, and they were paying attention and smiling, laughing at what seemed like his jokes.

I felt the cousins holding me and I felt the dull knife edge saw across my neck and I felt—I feel it again now, remembering—that electric sting, the hot blood on my skin, the panicked slap of my hand on the wound.

And later I showed my mom the cut at lunch but didn't say how it happened and my mom said, *What happened, a stick?* and I said, *Yeah, a stick*, and then she put a napkin against my neck. She lifted the napkin and looked every couple of minutes until the bleeding stopped, said, *Some stick. Careful.*

Then this image: it was hours later and I was standing in the parking lot at dusk and the black man with glasses in a sweat-stained gray shirt was laughing with all the other black boys and young men as they loaded their basketballs and bags into a clean, new, white church van that had written on its side the Holy Redeemer something something Church of Christ. I must have been with my mom and dad and brothers but they aren't in the memory. It's just me at the end of a hot day with a raw, pink cut on my neck and dirt-stained everything and the sky is gray-blue with a distended pink belly.

I am staring at the man and patting gently at my neck. He shuts the van doors. He walks toward me and asks if I am okay and I say, *Yeah I am except my neck got cut out in the woods*, and the man says he likes to use Bactine on his cuts—I remember this very clearly—even though it burns a little at first but the cut goes away faster and that is usually all there is to it. *Good as new. You can get it down at the drug store. Give you some, son, if I had it, but we left the aid kit at church.*

I look at the man. He is smiling. I want to say that I got my throat cut because I wouldn't yell a racist insult at him, but I don't know what racism is and don't have the language and don't know how. Talking. Other people. Me back then. I might as well have been trying to rebuild a car engine or do particle physics.

Before the man gets in the van and drives away, he says, *God bless you, son.* He says it like it's nothing, like I just sneezed. Then he pats me gently on the shoulder and looks into me. A second. Two seconds. Brown eyes and blue eyes. Nothing much. Why even remember this?

But in my dad's '65 Mustang, on the way home, my mom turns around and says, *Why are you crying, what's wrong, is something wrong?* and I say, *It's my neck, my neck hurts*, and my mom says, *We'll take care of it honey, we will, just calm down*, but it's not my neck, or the anger and shame and helplessness I feel because of my cruel and stupid cousin Kevin, who could have done anything he wanted to me—beaten me delirious, tied me up, held me to the ground. I don't know what it is. Exhaustion, the long day, the plastic picnic knife, my white family, those black boys and men, the squalor of the poor neighborhoods near the park turning slowly and darkly now in the car windows, a hand on my shoulder, a blessing at dusk. The world expands every day. Words barely touch it. And now my heart has opened like a sieve and I cannot hold back its tiny flood.

New Shoes, 1975

I'M ON MY HANDS AND KNEES, looking side to side beneath the tattered bus seats. In front of me are new white tennis shoes, size three or four, and above them frayed and yellowed socks, and above the socks a young girl's thin brown ankles.

What else?

Other brown ankles, other shoes, but none are this close, this bright, this white, this *new*. Metal bus-seat poles bolted to the black, filthy floor line up into the near distance like centipede legs. Why am I on the ground?

Follow the images. Try to remember.

I'm five, riding in the front of the school bus my mother drives every day through the Pine Chapel "projects" of Hampton, Virginia. She is in her early thirties, pregnant with my younger brother. It is seven years after the Fair

Housing Act made it illegal to use federal money to further racial segregation. The two of us are the only white people on the bus, and she is one of the only white people in the school system at the moment who will drive an all-black bus or do a route through Pine Chapel. Behind us are about fifty of the poorest African American kids in the state, kindergartners to eighth graders, kids whose families have been, over time, segregated out and cordoned off into heavily policed and impoverished government housing while we live in a small, tidy house in a nearby white neighborhood signed for by my father on credit and a guaranteed loan backed by that same government. Each weekday morning and afternoon in 1975, only a few years after major desegregation lawsuits, I sit by myself in the first loose, spring-creaking chair behind Mom's driver's seat, legs dangling, listening to the talk, the laughing, and the cursing of the kids. Language is a marvel—almost a solid material for building thought, memory, fantasy. Most of my life—everyone's lives?—is in my own head. *Such a good boy*, people say. *So quiet*. But my mind is a rapids, anything but quiet.

I've dropped something—a coin, one of the plastic toy figures of Batman or Aquaman I always had with me then, something—and now I'm on my hands and knees to pick it up. I can see all the way to the teal, steel back of the bus. But it's these shoes that draw my eye. Cheap, white, new.

Shoes have meaning. Shoes tell a story. Not how I think, of course, not at five—I'm about fourteen years from studying at university and first hearing the words "semiotics" and "ethnography" and "poststructuralism" and "commodity fetishism"—but something I seem to know because the teenage boys in my neighborhood wear blue Puma Clydes, or bright white Adidas Stan Smiths with three green stripes, or blue and yellow Nike running shoes with tan knobby soles. They parade these shoes, they runway-fashion-stroll them; every day I can see the boys belong together because of their shoes. There are other things that connect them as well—medium-length, feathered hair parted in the middle, T-shirts screen printed with words like "Cheap Trick" and "Foghat" and "Jethro Tull" and "Pink Floyd," their white skin. But it's the shoes that really *mean*, or so it seems, and it is cheap canvas shoes, what the teenage boys call "butter cookies," that can truly damn a person, subject them to the cruelest words, bullying. My mother drives a school bus. My father works at the nearby shipyard. Money is tight, our family never has enough (none of which do I know or understand), but I wear Nikes and if I didn't I would be poor white trash like my neighbors the Heeleys.

So when I get up from the bus floor—maybe with a plastic Batman in hand—I look back at the girl, at her face, then the older boy sitting beside her—her brother, I think—then the girl again. She does not look me in the eye. Her glasses are thick, plastic, cheap; her downcast eyes are magnified like a fish in the corner of an aquarium, like an image on a squeezed balloon. She is small, skinny. About my age— five, maybe six. Her black hair is parted in the middle with two tight braids. I would like her to look at me. For the first time on this bus, I have something important to say to one of the black kids.

Before I got my Nikes, before my mother relented to my begging for Nikes, the older boys in the neighborhood laughed at my shoes every day when they walked by as I rode my yellow, plastic skateboard with the translucent, rubber-cement-colored wheels on my short driveway and the thump-tump uneven sidewalk in front of my house. They said my mother drove the *midnight taxi* or *the prison bus*. They said, *Check tike's kicks*, or, *Nice moccasins, ke-mo-therapy,* then laughed, pushing each other. I didn't understand exactly what they meant, or why my white canvas shoes from Kmart that my grandmother bought me were such a joke, but I felt the sting from their comments, their laughing, went inside. *No more skateboarding?* said Mom. *Nah*, I said, then sat on the flowered couch in the small, dim living room in the silence and the tea-stain light and the boredom (time felt so big at five, like an ocean to swim through, like having your eyes open while you slept, the hours a dark, unmoving sludge). I looked down at my shoes. Such crap, crap shoes. Butter cookies. But then Christmas came and I wanted only one thing and I got my blue Nikes.

I am leaning over the back of the seat now. The girl and her brother and I are face-to-face inside the roaring tunnel of the bus. Did I have meanness in me as a kid? Certainly some, maybe plenty, but it's hard to know, really, since the child's mind is the adult's story, a thing I'm making on this laptop, a tale we tell ourselves to grant some meaning to and approximate our pasts, but I remembered, that day, the older white boys laughing at my shoes, celebrating a new thing wrong with me. A hurt thing wants to hurt. That much we all must know.

I say only two words: *Nice shoes*; then I laugh, my best neighborhood cool-kid derisive—like *spitting* on those embarrassing no-brand shoes.

The boy beside the girl, her brother, is the bus monitor. He helps my mother keep a lid on potential violence, which hums in the air some days. (My father believes the poor—and he has been at the edge of poor for most of his life—will fight to the finish over scraps, can be murderous over wounded pride, will steal useless things because useless things are still a kind of ownership and one notch up from nothing at all, and he does not like that my mother has agreed to do this and doesn't have a better, safer job—the grocery store, helping out at a white preschool—that his low salary reduces freedom, forces them to make choices they don't want to make.) The girl's brother is like my mother's fight cop. Mom says he is a gentleman, going somewhere. "No fights" is her one remaining rule. *Wanna fight?* he says to kids, standing up, eyeing them. *Get off the bus and kill each other. Nobody cares. Police don't care. Save their ass a bullet. But no fighting on the white lady's bus.*

He scowls. I think he must share my opinion of the girl's shoes—I assume everyone understands that she should be wearing Nikes, not those sad $2.99 Kmart specials. This is inviolable logic. I learned it from the cool white boys in my neighborhood.

He doesn't laugh. Instead he leans in toward me. I look at him, listen. I'm still smiling. He helps my mother. He can be trusted. He looks at his younger sister, who never talks, who holds his hand at the bus stop, who sits with him every day, sometimes right up against him, holding his arm, her head on his shoulder, then he looks at her new shoes, which still smell of pressed rubber and canvas, of the caved-in box they shipped in with a hundred other identical pairs. Quietly, through gritted teeth, so my mother cannot hear, he says, *What are you laughin' at? I bought them damn shoes. I'd take off one and beat your little ass with it, your momma weren't sitting right there. Turn around, boy, 'fore I slap your face.*

Little electric shock goes right through my forehead and all around inside my skull, staticking every thought. I turn around. Heart a marcher's snare. I hold my picked-up toy, Batman or Aquaman, tight in both hands. I cross and recross my shins, as if to hide my expensive Nikes.

At home I lie sock-footed on the flowered couch and watch Tom and Jerry wordlessly torture and terrorize each other to up-tempo piano music and exclamatory tuba sounds. I do not mention to my mother what happened on the bus, what the girl's brother said. The next day, walking out of the slappy screen door of the house for the morning route, she asks why I am not wearing my new shoes.

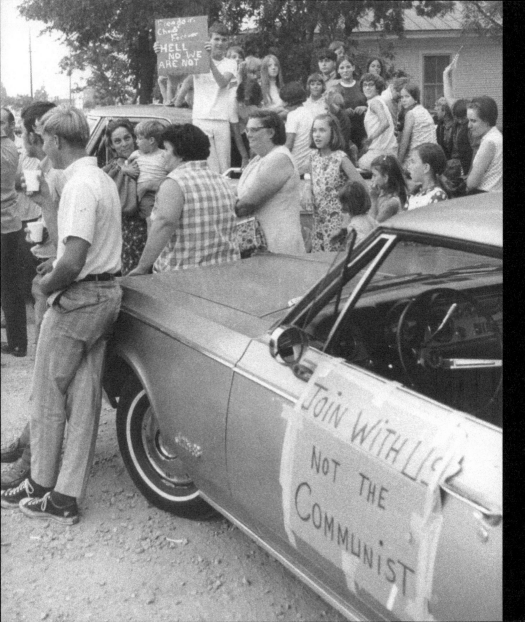

HOLY SHIT.

My neighbor Rodney Dean said that—I think—or maybe his older brother Kip. One of them. But I remember staring into the bullet hole in the car's driver's side door, six inches below the window, a few inches forward from the door handle. Rodney is thirteen. Kip is eighteen, and this is his metal-flake blue Chevelle in front of me, in the Deans' cracked, weed-sprouting driveway. I'm seven. Nineteen seventy-seven. (Put down what feels like the facts without literary fuss, maybe worry about style later.) I'm next door to hear the story of the shooting because this house, this family, this junk-strewn yard—storyville.

For instance:

The earth was made by God in six days about six thousand years ago.

Cutting your hair if you are a woman is a sin.

Showing your legs if you are a woman is a sin.

Wearing pants instead of long dresses or skirts if you are a woman is a sin.

Talking to a strange boy if you are a girl is a sin.

Men can punish women, in public, physically, for their sins.

I have seen the father, the snaggle-toothed, wrinkled mechanic, the amateur evangelist, beat each of his four daughters with a belt or a switch in the front yard (his four boys, too, but that seems less odd to me because corporal punishment is normal for boys in all the families that I know). We live in God's dominion, according to Mr. Dean, and the chosen shall lead us into being a fully Christian nation, not one filled with communists and dope fiends and queers. Also according to Mr. Dean: The black kids in the neighborhoods nearby are like roving platoons from an enemy army. Whites made this country. It is a white, Christian country. Whites must take it back. In Jesus' name. Amen.

Holy shit.

So now I get the story (there I am, the listener, hands in dungaree pockets), but have a hard time following the plot. Act 1: Rachel, the middle girl, fourteen, went into the Pine Chapel projects by herself because she had a friend from her class who lived there. The friend, of course, was black. She knows not to go there. She goes anyway. The friend had an older brother and some cousins and maybe strangers living with her and her grandma. Someone on the school bus told Rodney, the younger brother, that Rachel had a black boyfriend. Act 2: Big joke on the bus, repeated over and over: white girl, black boy. Rodney told Kip but didn't tell his dad. Act 3: Dusk came. A cold night. Kip went out in his Chevelle, picked up some friends—two, three; I don't clearly hear this part—and they drove through Pine Chapel with bats and crowbars. They drank beer after beer and got braver. Black teens on the corners watched them roll by once but not again. Second time Kip's friend started yelling. N-word this, N-word that. Another of Kip's friends flashed a pistol. Then from the other side of the road a loud bang, driver's side door *pinging* like a shot beer can. Right then a group of twenty, thirty kids come running around the corner, figures under the street lights, and Kip and the white boys are burning rubber and back home in a few minutes. Act 4: Rachel arrives home, an hour late and after lying about where she went. No boyfriend, just a friend, a girl, *Yes a black friend but we had a project to do. I had to. It was for school. I promise. I promise.*

Now is Act 5: I think I understand. Maybe I don't. The timing of all this is bunched up like thoughts, like words, like memories. Kip and Rodney are still talking, half joking, half fighting. I watch. The thing I must do in life, I understand, is pay attention, follow along.

Here is Mr. Dean with his pepper crew cut, his crooked teeth, his gray, cracked fingers, pushing his daughter Rachel by the neck out into the yard, to the car. *You see that?* he shouts. *See that?* She says, *Yes,* she does, she does see it, but she only went to do a project for school and Kip didn't have to come after her and drive around like that with music blaring and his friends shouting at people out the windows. *Those people live there*, Rachel says. *Her grandma cleared a table for us. She made us snacks.*

Mr. Dean slaps the back of Rachel's head and her never-cut hair whips like a clotheslined dress in the wind. *All because of your evil ways*, Mr. Dean says, pointing at the bullet hole with one hand and vice-gripping her neck with the other. *Stay with your kind*, he repeats as the swinging starts up again. Kip and Rodney and I watch as their father beats Rachel with the force of worship.

Incident at the Pool, 1977

I WATCHED THEM RIDE UP on their ramshackle, tacked-together, junkyard bikes, growing in size like spreading shadows out of the dark woods: five or six black teenage boys from Pine Chapel. They rode toward me (toward my perceptions and assumptions) and perched themselves—one shoe on a pedal, one on the pine-needled ground, handlebars turned parallel to frames—outside of the fence of Briar Station Pool, one of the many all-white pools in Hampton with no specific rules on the books regarding race, which would have been illegal if most likely not enforced. My mother had scraped together the little extra money she had to join this place and bring me here to swim, a five-minute walk from our house, every sunny summer day when I was five, six, and seven. I'd overheard both kids and parents at the pool say things about my mother being a bus driver—not judgmental things but delivered in a tone of judgment—because evidently her job was work most people wouldn't do.

In a lawn chair, towel around my neck, hair blackened wet, I held my snack—a Chick-O-Stick? a Charleston Chew?—sat statue-still, as if watching all this on TV, and stared at the tall kid closest to the fence.

He wore cut-off jeans and basketball shoes. No shirt. Black nipples; bony, brown ribcage. Little scars discolored to white-person skin. He and the rest of the boys had pantyhose on their heads, like toboggans (this image—so new to me then, so *foreign*—seems somehow the core of this memory, and every encounter I had had to this point was with (1) lower-middle- and working-class white people, (2) poor white people, and (3) poor black people). Here were signifiers of abject urban poverty, translated, in my young mind, into all the social stereotypes about poor black young men I'd heard and ingested, as if conjured from the woods behind the riders. And it would be years before I began to understand the massive black poverty around me back then in Hampton Roads—represented by this thick fence and this kid's half-ravaged torso and my perception that "black" and "poor" were synonymous—was an inevitable outcome of national and state history, laws, and policies, a number of which (education, finance, policing) were directly benefitting me, right down to our brick house (easy loan my father would not have received if he were black, a real estate agent who showed him the house because we were the right kind of family) and the chlorinated water dripping from my skin (new pipes in this neighborhood).

The boys sat on their bikes in the shade, sweating. It was ninety-five degrees, and they looked longingly at the arctic-ice-blue water of the pool. The boy who seemed to be the leader looked at me in my chair on the other side of the fence. He held up one finger from the handlebar, casually nodded his head.

Hot, he said.

I couldn't form thoughts or words.

Don't worry, he said. *We're just resting. Everything ain't a problem. Everything in the world ain't a problem.*

They rested like that for a couple of minutes. Then Johnny Segal jogged over. I thought, for a long time, his name was Johnny Seagull. I wanted a name like that—Greg Bear or Greg Coyote or Greg Eagle. Johnny was a big teen, athletic, captain of the swim team. He had hair on his chest, muscles. More hair climbed out of the front of his Speedo swimsuit. A sparkling diamond earring bull's-eyed his left earlobe. He looked like a pop star from the cover of *Teen* magazine.

More boys got out of the pool, came over dripping.

Suddenly it was eight, ten white teens on one side of the fence, five or six black teens on the other side. And I was still sitting in a chair, watching.

What are you looking at? said Johnny to the kid in the front of the bike riders, the one who talked to me.

The water, man, said the leader, *it's two hundred damn degrees.*

Nah. Nah, said Johnny. *No way.* He looked back at the water. *Why don't you get out of here. Ride off wherever you came from. Nothing for you here, man. Nothing to see.*

Crowd of skinny white boys behind Johnny, in swim suits, blisters of pool water on their skin, went, *Yeah, right, unh huh.*

These your woods? said the leader to Johnny. *Are you telling me I don't have a right to sit on my bike on a summer afternoon in some shade and look where I want to look?*

Not here, said Johnny. *Go somewhere else.*

Like I said, said the leader, *I don't think it's your call. Don't mind us, man. Everything ain't a problem. Go back to your swimming. We'll go when we've cooled off a bit.*

Briar Station was mostly moms and kids, a place for working-class whites to feel like they were part of a country club, socially higher than someone, something, though it wasn't upscale at all, only neat and clean and functional.

There was a long pause, staring. Bowed-up, adrenalined kids on both sides of the fence.

Then Johnny said, *I'm telling you to get out of here.* Then he called them all the N-word, which hit them fast and all at once like a blast from a firehose.

From one of the boys on the bikes behind the leader flew thrown mud like shrapnel, freckling the white skin of Johnny and the others.

What happened next? What else do I remember?

Commotion. Movement. Voices. The slap of bare feet on hot concrete. Johnny Seagull and the others racing past, out the main fence exit, toward the woods, to the spot from which the bike riders had already vanished.

A few weeks later I was skateboarding in my driveway with my neighbor Pete, who was older than me, maybe ten or eleven. We were practicing 360-degree spins. You needed to know how to do a 360 in my neighborhood in 1976, '77.

It was the end of summer, all the grass scorched brown, the dusks redder now, days shortening. Men washing cars. Sprinklers. Led Zeppelin out of some kid's dark bedroom window.

Pete told me to be careful if I ever went to the pool. He said that gangs of black kids on bikes wearing pantyhose masks were riding along the fences now and throwing rocks at swimmers, at mothers and little babies. He said he heard they carried knives and shouted curse words even at the preacher's wife.

I stopped spinning my board around, put one foot down. I looked at him, squinting. I had been swimming at the pool every nice day all summer. Nothing had happened since the day Johnny called the black kids resting in the shade that word. Just quiet summer. White kids swimming in the mind-blanking Virginia heat. Wiggling, sun-scaled blue like a Popsicle or an iris. Wind in the trees. Chlorine burn in my nose and eyes and throat. Rise and fall of water against concrete sides. White kids yelping as they came off the diving boards. Other white kids cheering them on. White moms watching, tanning, reading magazines. I'd almost forgotten about the incident.

But over time, into the fall, into the winter, something about Pete's lie burrowed down into me, changed me for a while. Language, stories, the mind—they can morph like unstable information or the colors of daylight until they settle around acceptable meaning. And when you're young, a blank slate, you especially need stories, need the stories of your community to anchor you, tell you who you are.

I had felt mostly a vague shame about the day Johnny Seagull called the black kids that name before I heard Pete's story. I remembered how the boy on his bike had raised a finger to say hello. I remembered him talking to me, talking to me like anybody else would (like a white person, I would have thought back then). And I thought the boy on the bike was right, about the shady woods being a free place for anyone, from anywhere, to rest. Months later, though, I began to understand we neighborhood kids were part of something bigger, this unspoken apartheid, a reality so plain and present it took the magic of American myth-making to make its causes vanish each second of every day; I felt sometimes, at that point, like a cop or a soldier of my block, conscripted into some amorphous battle I didn't really understand. By then I was telling Pete and any kid who would listen about the day I was just minding my own damn business and having a snack during pool break when some crazy kids from the projects almost killed me with thrown rocks.

Thumb, 1975

THIS MEMORY IS STUCK like a deep splinter of experience in my mind.

Perhaps my favorite friend in kindergarten was black. His name was Barry Fox. Funny kid. Elementary comedian. And very, very dark. His five-year-old skin was the color of walnut wood stain still in the can. I thought it was cool, his skin. Amazing, actually. I didn't think of my skin, which was pasty white and blotched with freckles and would later be a veritable garden for skin cancer, as having any color beyond *normal* or *regular American*. I didn't yet understand, at five, why we didn't even ask to go to each other's birthdays, or that his skin made him worth less than me at Robert E. Lee Elementary, the South, and America. (The two of us walking in the front doors of a school named after a Confederate general would be so clumsily ironic as to strain credulity if this were fiction.)

One day in 1975, goofing around in Mrs. Smith's class, doing funny voices, slapsticking a fake fall, *whoa whoa whoooooaaaaa*, Barry accidentally tipped his desk over and smashed his middle finger. Blood curdling screams. Everyone looking. Mrs. Smith running over. I have this out-of-time image in my mind of a blond woman in a white dress, on her knees, on the ground, beside a tipped over desk, holding a panicked black child as he squeezes one hand with the other, huffing, gritting teeth, huffing. Then another image of Barry's brown-black finger, the lighter color of his fingernails, and the one blue-purple nail, which would not have been apparent on that day but later—many days or even a week—when he was back in class, bandage-free, showing me the bulbous, blood-filled wound. But linear time is not the essence of memory. These images crowd around the event like iron filings pulled to a magnet.

At the end of the day, this kindergarten day, my grandmother, my mother's mother, is picking me up. Kids streaming toward the buses.

Hampton was about half white and half black when I lived there in the 1970s (it is majority black now). That's the basic makeup of the crowd, during busing and pre–white flight, as my grandmother and I walk the halls, head for the door. I look up. She's wearing her waitress uniform, has a small beige purse hanging from her forearm. She's in her early fifties. She has short, brown hair. She wears horned-rimmed glasses. I hear the *tap-squish* of her comfortable, white shoes, like a nurse's.

And what of this kid crowd? Just over a decade before, Robert E. Lee was an all-white school. Whites picketed integration all over the city, held up signs. "No Bus for Us." "Keep Schools White." "Not My Water Fountain." "Go Back to Your Neighborhood (Africa)." But now kids, black and white, laugh and skip and push each other with no knowledge of recent history. History and culture are the current we are all flowing along—and we all, black and white, feel it—yet we don't have the thoughts and the language to comprehend this moment, or this racially mixed crowd, or this small, forgotten instant in American education.

Walking by the main office, I see Barry through the glass. He's sitting on the low, pilled-up burgundy sofa outside the principal's door. The principal (the vice principal? the guidance counselor?) is a tall, white woman. She is on the phone on the other side of the glass, inside her office. Sharp, that woman. Every jutting bone a blade. Her hair is always pulled tightly back into a brown and gray bun. She parts the child-clotted day like the bow of a ship parts debris-filled water. She could glue that phone to the side of her head to save time for all those calls she has to make to parents, grandparents, guardians, relatives, social workers, cops. *God it's loud in these halls!*

I wave to Barry on the other side of the glass. My grandmother looks at him, too. The blackest black kid (let's not pretend that within a white supremacist framework unconscious bias does not become more pronounced as skin tone darkens). In an office of white people. He doesn't wave back.

He is hunched. He is, I see now, quietly crying. I expect from him some mime act of a hammer coming down on his finger, maybe his hand in a bear trap, something Three Stooges. But he's defeated, comedy free, this funny, funny kid whose deep darkness, in this Hopperesque painting of a tableau, draws the eye, stands out. I don't know why he is acting this way—surely they put ice on his finger— and my grandmother is pulling me by the hand, through the crowd, toward the car, in a hurry.

Barry missed school the next day. An organizing mental image I have related to this is Mrs. Smith, who I believe cared very much for Barry and me and all the other kids, black and white, telling the class in a professional but shaky voice that Barry was having a break from school for his unruly behavior.

The Pier, 1976

ON THE BUCKROE BEACH fishing pier, my other grandmother, my father's mother, is talking to an old black man
about the best bait to use for flounder fishing.

My grandmother and I are sitting on white five-gallon buckets,
a couple of feet from the wood-slat rails of the pier. Her rod
is perched between the top and second-to-the-top slats, her
fishing line dropping taut and straight into the brown and
barely moving Chesapeake Bay (a heavy sinker is used for
bottom-feeders like flounder).

She is between me and the old black man, who also has a
five-gallon bucket, but his is right-side-up and has four or
five croakers in it, along with some large minnows, so he is
standing.

I am sitting here with my grandmother in the bright sun, in
the dead-still day, in the ninety-degree humid heat, in hopes

of catching this elusive fish. Flounder are out, she says. Fish are biting. I have never caught a flounder, which can reach up to two feet in length in these waters and have both eyes on the tops of their heads. If I understand correctly, they are only in near shore, along the sandy beaches of Hampton—Buckroe and Grandview—a few times a year. This is one of those times.

I look around. Horseflies, black with green abdomens, contrail around in the heat and smell of sun-cooking fish rot. Off both sides of the pier people are fishing. Fifty, maybe sixty people. A third are white. Everyone else is black. Everyone here is working-class or poor, but I don't know or understand that, obviously—don't even know what that means beyond cheap shoes and small houses or trailers. Like look at my grandmother's shoes—white faux leather/plastic with two Velcro cinches. Like look at her old clothes bought cheaply from discount stores, look at how what other people might see when they look at her never enters her mind. Vanity is for people with money, people who own excess time to fill with superficial worries.

And what am I wearing? Who knows? I can't see myself in this memory.

And what else would poor mean to me at five?

Counting change too often.

Ashtrays full of cigarette butts no one thinks to empty.

A parking lot full of old cars and trucks, rusted bumpers, cardboard taped in a glass-gone window. My mamma's car that rattles and shimmies and burps smoke out of its tailpipe.

Having to ride the bus to work sometimes—with black people.

Now the black man gives my mamma some bait, a large live minnow, and a few tips after an hour of the two of us not catching a flounder.

Use a heavier sinker, he says. *Pin the live minnow down along the bottom, so he swims crazy near the sand-covered flounders.*

Half an hour later she catches one of the biggest flounders of the day. Everyone on the pier comes over to see the fish flopping on the dock. It is a marvel, brown and slimy on one side, with eyes like two small and yellow marbles mushed into clay, white on the belly.

I am so proud and happy my heart feels like a balloon and my ears ring a little. At five this is one more wild miracle in my stream of perceptions, and my days slide timeless into night dreams and back again.

My mamma is worried about the black people in Hampton getting so close to her neighborhood, taking over the schools. Her opinions are harsh and clear on these matters. Racist, sure, and absolutely common— white majority opinions. There are never any complicated or ambiguous ideas when I am in her world. She was complaining two hours ago in the pier parking lot, looking for a space. *Taking over*, she said.

But here is why I get caught up in this curious memory—she and this old man are giving each other high fives and laughing and talking and getting to know each other like they are about to become best friends. The crowd is black and white, everyone happy and together around this fish, exchanging supportive words, smiles. Fifteen minutes of seeming harmony in the place of the first black American slave, a thriving KKK, Massive Resistance, marches against busing, school closings just to keep black children out.

And for a long time after this—maybe years—she, a poor, old white woman, with off-and-on issues of depression and alcoholic self-medicating, and he, an old black man with who knows what kind of life and joys and pains, *are* the best of friends—for a couple of hours at a time, many Saturdays, as long as they are on that pier and have fishing poles in their hands.

Please Save Our
Neighborhood Schools
We Will Fight
For Our Constitutional
Rights
Our Children Will Not Be
Bused

ON THE WHITE-KID BUS—my neighborhood bus—Jerry's favorite subject in the fall of 1976, when I am in first grade, is the coming race war, which is going to start at Eaton Junior High and Robert E. Lee Elementary next week.

Jerry is eleven maybe. He's friends with my older brother. He looks like the older brother on *Eight Is Enough*, a forthcoming TV show. He kind of looks like Danny Partridge, another older brother on a TV show that isn't on anymore but was good, as good as *The Monkees* maybe, but certainly no *Batman*. Television shows and older brothers and cool sneakers and carefully messy haircuts and pop music and screen-printed T-shirts are comfortable and accessible reference points, and in many ways will be for the rest of my life. I am, I think, in every way cobbled together, American-made.

Jerry tells stories. He talks all the time (my core visual memory of him is his long, thin face and his pink-purple lips moving at fast-forward video speed). He is a word spigot, mostly a fountain of lies—and everyone knows it, everyone rolls their eyes, calls BS. Yet he talks and we are rapt. He has the slick delivery of a future racist demagogue. The information is all twisted in a dark direction, but the performance is smooth and captivating and we can't not listen. Could he be right?

He is turned around in his seat, talking down—literally speaking downward—toward me and my neighbor Steve, the kid with the awesome pellet gun, which my mom won't let me play with but sometimes I play with anyway. Jerry says last year on Hell Day—Halloween—a bunch of black girls broke the leg of a white girl. He says that at the end of school that same day a black boy tried to knife a white boy. This year black kids plan to kill someone. *Swear to God.*

And now I remember asking my older brother—my now dead older brother as I write this—if he's ever heard of Hell Day.

Yeah, he says. He is on the driveway, with his cool, midlength blond hair and those awesome sneaks and he's only just started down a road of narcotics and mental illness and his mind isn't yet a horror show. He says, *Everyone has heard of Hell Day. Thing is, it's always supposed to happen but it never happens. Some kids say stuff, maybe push each other. Someone told you it was going to happen this Halloween, didn't they?*

Yeah.

Who?

Jerry.

Jerry? That guy's an idiot and a liar. Look, you gotta watch out for blacks [no one says "blacks," "black people," or "African Americans"], *especially when there are a bunch of them together and only a few whites, and never go into a black neighborhood. They could definitely beat your ass. But Hell day? That's just something people talk about to keep the drama going.*

Drama?

Just neighborhood crap. City crap. School crap. It's a story about how black people have ruined everything and white people don't even want to go to the damn schools around here anymore. Rich kids go to private schools now. Half the families in the neighborhood are trying to move to the country. Just let the blacks have these rotten schools is what people think now.

This is puzzling. Chest-squeezing. I love school. Half of my first grade class is white and half is black, like my city. Barry Fox, who is really, really black, is probably the coolest kid I know. I have a platonic crush on him! And I've never thought of being scared at school until now, after Jerry's story.

That Halloween when I go into Robert E. Lee, into my first grade class, to the gym, the lunchroom, the playground, the library, it is a little like how I feel after watching a scary movie. I know a ghost isn't going to come out from behind a door, know nothing is going to happen.

I know Jerry is a liar.

I know Hell Day is rumors and gossip.

Only this new fear is real.

MY FAMILY GOES to Sammy & Nick's Steak House every Friday night. The place has a $2.99 Burger Boat—big cheese burger, huge helping of greasy fries. All five of us (Mom, Dad, me, my two brothers) eat—no sodas, no desserts—for just over $15. I look forward to this weekly dinner out. It's what middle-class people do.

One night a giant black man walks in. He stands at the hostess's desk. He's smiling. He's six and a half feet tall. He wears a brown, corduroy blazer, the jacket as big as a couch cover. He looks like a football player, a sports star. He's about my dad's age, mid-thirties. He looks at our table. His eyes show recognition. I think he's looking at me. I look down at my burger. A rush of blood goes to my head. I look, carefully, back up toward the entrance. Then, in a loud voice, the black man says, *Hey, R.B.* (which is what most people call my dad). He walks over and stands beside our table. My dad is looking up at the man, smiling. He wipes grease and ketchup off of his fingers with a napkin and then shakes the man's hand.

Hey, Claude, my dad says, swallowing. *Nice to see you, man.*

Claude's wife and daughter are behind him. His wife is white, blonde. His daughter is tan with green eyes and black wavy hair. She is pretty. And have I ever seen a white wife with a black husband? I don't think so, and though I don't know this, such a thing has only been legal in Virginia—a holdout state, a Southern state against so-called miscegenation—since 1967, when *Loving v. Virginia* was settled in the Supreme Court. The families meet each other. *Hi. Hi. Hello. How are you?*

Claude says, *Hey, R.B., do that bird call you do for my wife. I've told her about it. I told her what a good guy you are and how you keep our spirits up down in our dungeon at the shipyard. This is him, Cheryl, our department's comedian. R.B.!*

Nah, Claude, says my dad. *Not here.* He looks at us around the table. His face is pinking.

Oh, come on, R.B. I've told her all about it. I've tried to describe it but I really can't; you have to hear it for yourself, don't you? I mean you really have to hear it to appreciate it.

My dad thinks about it, looks around. He wipes both hands on his napkin again. He takes in a breath. My mom and two brothers and I watch him in silence. He puts his thumb and third finger on either corner of his mouth. He pushes his lips wide, and I can see the tip of his pink, tightly curled tongue against his top lip.

Suddenly my dad lets out a crazy looping and dancing whistle, a shrill vibrato that sails around the room like a laughing flock of tropical birds. I've never heard anything like it. I can't believe it came out of my no-nonsense dad.

All the other diners—twenty-five or thirty people—stop eating and stare at my dad. Sudden quiet. My head feels heavy. I hear my heart. Then all I hear is the strangely high-pitched laughter of Claude. Claude's wife is smiling. Claude's daughter is smiling. I think I might be, uncomfortably, smiling.

See, Claude says to his wife. *See? I told you old R.B. was a card, the life of the party. Yes, he is. Yes, indeed, he is. Well, listen, enjoy your burger, R.B., and best to you all. Nice to meet you.* He pats my dad's back. *See you on Monday, R.B.* He touches him again, a hard pat on and then squeeze of the shoulder.

Yeah, Claude, my dad says. *See you on Monday down in the dungeon.*

After Claude leaves, still laughing, my mom says, *Was that him?*

Yeah, my dad says, and goes back to eating.

There is a long silence. Chewing.

I ask, *Who was that man? How do you know him?*

My mom says, *He works with Dad. He's from up north.*

He's your boss?

My dad's face looks hot. He's almost sweating. He continues eating, looking down at his messy plate of special-priced food.

My older brother says, *Is he a boss, Dad?*

My dad finishes chewing. He looks up now, at each of us. He says, *Look, Claude's an alright guy, a friend from work, but he's not my boss. Now can we be quiet and finish our food?*

I WALK INTO my grandmother's kitchen. My face is slightly higher than the beige apron bow on her back.

This kitchen is small, with a metal-edged, rusty-legged, vinyl-topped table pushed against the wall. A corner of the floor curls like whittled wood scrap. The cabinets are dull white. The screen in the aluminum door to the gravel driveway grays and crosshatches the day. I brush up against my mamma's blue polyester pants. She looks down, noticing me, her helper, sent in by her son, my father. And here—just after the grabbing sensation of polyester against my bare arm and seeing her face above—is the sensory memory of the smell pulling me back through years, like a gush. Raw hog's intestines. I hold my nose—then and now.

Put your hand down, she says, leaning over, working with her hands in the sink, which I can't see. She pulls, kneads, squeezes. Grease reaches to her elbows like a pair of glistening, translucent gloves. She faces out the double window, into thick, slow morning light, toward the dirt patches in her front yard and the neighbor's white clapboard house across the street and a clothes-strewn line in someone's backyard in the black neighborhood one block over. (Black people are getting closer to her street each year, like a rising tide, she says, and more and more of her neighbors who can afford it are moving away—to small, all- or mostly white cities and towns like Gloucester, Yorktown, Poquoson.)

In a metal bucket out back, near the rusted oil tank, in the tall grass and mosquito-swarming heat, Mamma has already done a rough cleaning of the chitlins, her round-bellied mutt, Purty Girl, sniffing around for scraps. She knows poor preparation is sure sickness— cramps, vomiting, yellow eyes, a fever. *There is a* right *way*, she says. *I am showing you the right way.*

She pushes her hand through a long piece of small intestine, making it a sleeve, and pulls it inside out. She picks fat, remnants of the hog's last meal, maybe bits of feces. She finds polyps and small benign tumors like hard BBs, cuts them out with a paring knife. Finally, she chops the cleaned meat into one-inch pieces.

Washing her hands, she says, *Now watch. Pay attention.*

She fries onion halves in pork fat in the bottom of a ten-pound pot, dumps in the intestine meat, covers it in water, adds cider vinegar, Tabasco sauce, chunks of potato, peppers from her garden. She will stew the chitlins all morning and afternoon, then serve them at dinner (which is in the afternoon) with collard greens, fried chicken, and buttermilk biscuits.

I know now (writing, a professor), but did not know then (existing, a kid), that she was telling me, in her way, this was part of who we are—white Southerners in an increasingly crime-ridden city and good Protestants from sturdy, hard-working farm stock and the great state of Virginia by way of eastern North Carolina. You should waste nothing, ever—not a scrap. You should learn about your family, how they once raised hogs and how she learned all this preparation procedure from her mother and sisters. After the hog slaughter in December every year when she was a girl and her family were migrant farmers up and down the fertile Piedmont, the young women of the farm would be to their shoulders in blood, working, making all this death into life for the family.

But I am a child, more curious about the mystery in the sink than the cooking pot, the recipe, its connection to my family's American past stretching back in time. What could any of this history mean to me today, in this sun-filled kitchen, at seven years old?

When she leaves the room for a moment—*Don't touch anything*—I kneel on a wobbly kitchen chair, see the remnants of the preparation in the sink—pink hunks, white globular flecks, the compost of it all. I become scared, at that moment, of my grandmother, her house, her strange folk ways. The smell is weight, pressure, like standing in a backed-up public restroom, the mind blanked by sensation, like the ill feeling of an untethered memory's churn in the middle of the night. *Where am I?*

My family lives nearby, in the small brick house, but in a neighborhood in the changing New South that seems somehow decades away from this house and street. I like skateboarding and finding cigarette butts by the drainage ditch behind my house; I like playing video games at the new arcade in the strip mall or the 7-Eleven; I like shooting my best friend's pellet rifle, which he used, he swears, to kill a bird once. Much more than to be saved by Jesus, which is the only talk at our Methodist church, I want a pair of green or navy Pumas and the new Tom Petty and the Heartbreakers album that my older brother and his friends have.

At seven I cannot, of course, process these disparate existences, and this *feeling of confusion* is why, no doubt, the memory will persist decades from this moment, roiling and reshaping itself. I'm caught—without knowing or understanding—in the change from bucolic to urban and suburban, from local to global trends, from Jim Crow and complete racial segregation to the continuing attempts at educational integration, more equality for black people, blocks changing from white to white/black to black. My mamma kills animals and eats their entrails like some kind of witch or— Jerry says—some country N-word. Her reality, in her South, has always been about survival and work in the here and now so she can continue on. To her, all acts need to be sensible, practical; to me, hers is a life, compared to the flux and flow of information all around me, which seems stunted, bewildering. She knows better than to pine for what she cannot have, to put any stock in silly dreams, which will only crush you and make you crazy. But my world—a much, much faster, mediated world (even in the relative-to-now late 1970s)—will soon enough be all about chasing dreams and desiring the unlikely, watching television and movies and acquiring stuff and attitude and consumer and celebrity fantasies, a rock 'n roll shuffle, and then learning how to feign toughness, coolness, and sexual knowledge for other boys. I will try to get rid of this embarrassing Southern boy accent and these odd rituals (I'd really like one of those rock 'n' roll British accents!). I will want to be accepted, worldly. To be something new, I will, for a time, have to reject—really *deny*—everything old.

In the car, on the way home, my father scolds me for refusing to try the chitlins, telling me angrily my mamma made them special.

But my father ran away from this past, too, I will understand years later, tried to make it disappear. As an adult, he strived and struggled for and finally achieved a precarious and later more solid middle-class existence, a sense of dignity, a little respect. He would not be a poor "redneck," he would not be indicted by outside assumption, which he had seen all through his childhood was a curse for his mother and dead father, a mark of failure, coarseness, ignorance, and a relegation to the margins. He later regretted the way he had turned his back on everything. He had lost part of what was essential, a full acceptance of the people he loved. He was, this day, bringing me back to some kind of complicated origin. But I didn't, couldn't see it.

As I write, with my mamma and father both long dead, I vividly see the scene in the kitchen, a mix of memory and fiction, no doubt, moments pulled out of time. I want to bend their stories away from bleak bitterness, racial dynamics and determinism, class shame, and resentments toward a confusing and changing world. I want to make this memory of them about the resourcefulness of my ancestors, people who took scraps and learned how to turn them into something I can't seem to swallow and keep down.

The Student, 1961

MY MOTHER REMEMBERS the first black student admitted to Hampton High School. It was the late summer of 1961. His name was Robert Aaron Rice Jr. (she didn't remember this, I had to look his name up, but she did remember he was the son of faculty at historically black college Hampton Institute, now Hampton University). He was fifteen. My mother was seventeen.

This was six and a half years after the *Brown v. Board of Education of Topeka, Kansas*, Supreme Court ruling, which made systematic segregation along racial lines illegal, but my mother, my family, wouldn't have been focused on that, wouldn't have been thinking in any direct way about domestic policy or a legal case seemingly (only seemingly) so far from their lives. If the people around me when I was a kid—my family, neighbors—thought about the effects of Massive Resistance, the long racist legal battle in Virginia that set up impediments to racial integration through the courts, which

kept a person of color like Rice away from Hampton High for six long years after that Supreme Court ruling, they didn't mention it.

But my mother—because of her job driving the bus, or maybe because she believes in Jesus and His fight against suffering and injustice I hear each Sunday morning—has told me about the first black student at her school more than once. She said it was lonely. She didn't say Rice seemed lonely. Or she imagined he was lonely. She didn't place the loneliness anywhere—as if it were not the condition or mental state of a person, her or him, but more like a thin fog in the air, an American virus floating on a breeze. *Loneliness. Separation. Isolation. Outsiders and insiders. Us and them.*

She said he walked through the front doors of the school and down the main hallway. He wore a nice button-up shirt, pressed slacks, and shiny shoes. He had a sharp new haircut. He smelled faintly of cologne. He held his books close to his body, eyes forward, chin up, and walked quietly down the hall toward his classroom. He seemed calm, collected. She imagined he was filled with fear, but he didn't look afraid.

Unlike other places in the South, there were no major upheavals or violent protests (partly because Massive Resistance, backed by white supremacist governors and an all-white legislature, delayed integration for so long in Virginia that some of the hysterical, violent edge had come off of white resistance). There were small pockets of acceptance, bigger pockets of grudging acceptance, and still bigger pockets of seething resentment, prejudice, and fear, but integration went ahead.

She didn't remember any kids she knew saying "ugly things" about Rice. She just remembers how sharply dressed he was, how he walked so steadily and intently, not looking at anyone, his shoulders square. She remembers every white face, with the pattern of dominoes falling, turning to watch him walk by.

My mother tells me stories all the time. But this isn't a story. It's a fragment—just a description of a moment—because she doesn't fully understand what it means.

It was so lonely, she says. One teenager walking. Silence except for the shuffle of his feet. All the other teenagers watching him walk.

Shit

Goddamn

Get off your ass and dance

You peanut butter motherfuckin' two-ballin' bitch

Your momma's in the kitchen cookin' red-hot shit

Your daddy's in hell

Your brother's in jail

Your sister's 'round the corner singin' pussy for sale!

THAT'S THE SONG I SANG one day with some of the black kids in the back of the bus my mom drove. The bus was so loud she couldn't make out anything coming from the back. I don't remember how or why I was in the back of the bus. It's a memory without much immediate context. But the above verse was known as the "Pine Chapel song," and it was sung at full volume. Kids sang it as protest and comedy. It was poverty and violence and jail and death bent into revolt, gallows humor, and bus ride vaudeville.

Getting me, the white bus driver's kid, to sing it, sing it like I really meant it, like I lived it, like my future was as obstacle ridden and America-scorched and precarious and fined and court ordered and detained and longevity challenged as theirs, was the funniest thing they'd ever seen. *Watch this little white boy sing!*

We'd all finish the song and then laugh together in the back of the bus until we were snorting and delirious and in tears, high-fiving each other. Wipe your eyes. Take a breath. *Again! Again! Again!*

THIS KID BROUGHT a soldier's parachute from Vietnam to the church covered-dish supper. As I've said, my family was Methodist. I still believe—though I am no longer a steady churchgoer—in John Wesley's core idea that it is a person's deeds for which they should ultimately be judged. Maybe that's why this memory persists.

Here are ten, maybe twelve, boys in a sun-warm field. They're gathered around the parachute, which is laid out on the brown March grass, sprawling and rippled like a giant, beached octopus, canvas skin twitching in the wind gusts. One of the boys, a fifteen-year-old named Chuck (he hates—I remember—when his mom shouts "Charles" from the picnic area behind the red-brick church), has brought this to the covered-dish to show off. His father died in Vietnam. His stepfather has relegated his dad's war memorabilia to the attic, but Chuck's mom lets him rummage through and show off anything he wants. Today's show-and-tell is the parachute.

These covered-dish events are all about community, and I love them when I am six, seven, and eight the way I love God: unequivocally, uncritically, gratefully. Every soul here is white, and boys play tag, or basketball, or even tackle football—sometimes with girls! We eat Brunswick stew and soft, yellow rolls and then sticky fruit pies and melting ice cream. God is a part of all this, sure, but my dad can't stand Holy Rollers—people like our neighbors the dirty, crazy Deans, who are white trash as low as any poor people from the nearby housing projects—so he's chosen this church for its practicality and its sane and sober sermons, which seek to comfort and inspire aspirational white people like us rather than frighten them with promises of hell and punishment. My dad says that after a long week of hard work nobody needs to hear some sweating hick screaming hogwash about the end times.

This parachute wasn't Chuck's dad's. It was his dad's best friend's, who also died in the war. This man, Chuck says, was a hero. *He saved my dad's life more than once.* The two men were like brothers. *If you want,* Chuck says, *I'll get my mom to show you a picture of the two of them when we eat. To prove to you wingnut banana hammocks this ain't bullcrap.*

The games begin. We are all heroes now in the early spring sunshine, holding on to the chute's lines, the thing filling with March air, rising up, ballooning, pulling two or three or four boys along through the field, tumbling and knee-walking and butt-skidding toward the pine tree woods in the distance. I shout out as I am lifted up, tugged away from the church. I imagine the sounds of war because I have dropped behind enemy lines, bombs are exploding all around, bullets sing through the air near my ears. We are all the man who saved Chuck's dad's life that time, back before he got unlucky and died in some war not even a decade gone but already mostly a collection of one-liners spoken by deranged and shamed soldiers before explosions kill them in movie scenes.

Later, at supper, boys gather around Chuck's mother, a heavy redhead with boobs—according to one of the older boys—*out to here*. She gets out her purse, rummages for her wallet, a thick, card-filled thing that looks like tan pleather on a waiting-room couch.

Here it is, she says. *Have a look. You hold it, Charles.*

Chuck shows us the photo as we're gathered, jockeying for a better view, in a tight circle. The photo is faded, weathered, its edges tissue soft. It is two soldiers, in their mid-twenties, wearing green fatigues, each man's arm over the shoulder of the other, in front of a green, mud-splattered jeep. The smiling man is white. The laughing man is black.

Silence. A long pause. *Cool*, someone says, noncommittally. *So that's the hero, huh?* someone else says. *Pretty neat, Chuck. Cool. Totally cool. Very cool.*

After eating, a purpling Sunday dusk settling down on the church, Chuck says, *Hey, let's go get the parachute filled with wind again. I'll bet it can pull some of these pipsqueaks all the way across the field until the back pockets peel off their jeans.*

But no one is interested in the parachute anymore. The older boys are going to play one last game of basketball, Saints versus Crusaders. The younger boys are catching fireflies. I want to go back in the field with the parachute. I can't remember when I've had this much fun. I watch all the boys scatter quietly in different directions. Then I catch on, suddenly, and decide that catching fireflies has always been one of my favorite things to do.

The Field, 1977

THREE OR FOUR CARS get broken into in our neighborhood.

Someone saw a gang of black boys walking nearby. Not a group or a bunch. Language matters. Framing matters. A *gang*.

The black boys were not in our neighborhood, but they were *in the vicinity of our neighborhood*, close enough.

A gang of them?

What good could come of that?

What *else* might be missing?

Check all the yards, other cars, garages.

This afternoon I'm walking across the field behind the neighborhood. The field is the size of the mall parking lot, a sprawling, nearly perfect

rectangle. At the north end is our Methodist church, a brick building hoisting up a cross. It's winter, weak light, the sun a white bulb above a skeletal tree. Paper-thin ice on the surface of mud puddles.

That black neighborhood on one side of this field, just over there, is a foreign country to which I can never travel. I'd be robbed, beaten, maybe murdered. I know this. There is no space for doubt in these assumptions.

I'm moving now from the center of the field—the shortest walking distance toward my neighborhood—to the west side of the field, nearer to my home, though it is a longer walk because I must travel south along a fence and then around it and back north to the house, instead of at a more direct angle.

This field has become a no-man's-land, a moat, an imaginary wall, a psychically policed space between us and them, them and us.

Black people know this. White people know this.

I don't understand as I walk—I won't understand for a long time—but this is part of how racialized notions of crime work, continue to work. They are ideological, language-built. Transferrable through gossip, disseminated in mass media, visual and aural culture. Polished into fear. Injected into the social bloodstream. A virus inside the body politic.

I will grow up to revere words because all power starts with words. *In the beginning was the Word* . . . and in the end will be what? For the phenomenologist—and all humans are in the end phenomenologists—simply no more subjective sensations to make into words. Annie Dillard: "Significant as it was, it did not matter a whit. For what is significance? It is significance for people. No people, no significance. This is all I have to tell you."

If a black person commits a crime in or near our neighborhood, at the school, wherever, it is significant, iconic; it represents the ill intent of all black people, citywide, statewide, nationwide, worldwide. It is an incident and the potential start of an epidemic because every black person—in this way of believing and feeling—is part of an easily characterized black collective, a suspect demographic, regardless of where on this vast, globalized, multicultural planet he or she or they might come from or be.

The dominant white cultural mind—this social-psychological hive in the South in the 1970s in which I exist, invisible to itself—cannot make space for the individuality of an Other. (William James: "Now the blindness in human beings . . . is the blindness with which we all are afflicted in regard to the feelings of . . . people different from ourselves." Frantz Fanon: "There are too many idiots in this world. And having said it, I have the burden of proving it.")

An Other is a part of a group *only* and will act in a predictable way *as a part of that group*.

So white people, in my world, my past, cross the street to avoid black youths.

White police stop black youths because if they are not guilty of one thing, they are guilty of another thing. Black police do this, too, because the system is white even if you yourself, working in it, are black.

The black person is more often harshly sentenced, more often denied bail, more often accused with scant evidence, and more often imprisoned.

The white person is case by case—an individual (class and lack of resources—financial, educational, social, emotional—play a big part here).

The white person, the white kid, me, is conditioned to believe—partly because time faces us always forward, obscuring the past's damning evidence, and our subjectivity, our *phenomenological experience*, is such a tiny window, a pinhole really, on the world—that the poor black person brought all negative forces and outcomes on himself. The causes of history vanish like escalator stairs and it is hard work to think in the abstract, to make connections (abstract thought also takes significant educational and intellectual resources and privilege). At this point in time, I simply can't. Walking in this field, on this day in Virginia, in the South, in 1977, in this weak winter light that dulls all colors, I am incapable of pondering the strangeness of this situation in relation to other recent incidents, these double standards.

For instance, a neighborhood boy was arrested for possession of marijuana. Another boy stole money and electronics from his own house to buy drugs. Yet every white teen in my neighborhood is not assumed to be a drug addict. How absurd! How specious! How illogical! How racist!

And on the white-kid bus Jerry told me about how a boy the two of us know (or know of) raped a girl in the woods and now is in big trouble (I think, in 1977, rape is forcing someone to kiss you). No one makes the mental leap that all white males in my neighborhood are rapists. And years later when mass shootings start to happen all around the U.S., no one suggests—or even thinks?—young white males should be quarantined, monitored, kept from purchasing weapons. Surveilled! Rounded up! Deported!

If only I could imagine what racial dominance gets the white person, gets me.

Individuality, for one. Unquestioned agency, for another. Distinction from the demographic group, for yet another. All *without thought*.

I get to be a boy uncloaked by race because white is not a race or an ethnicity or a particular identity but the norm by which all else is judged, and thus invisible. I get to be a self not only in my own young mind but in the minds of those around me, those with power.

Today I—the little boy "I," the former me—look across the dead grass at the black neighborhood. Then I turn and step quickly toward home and what I believe to be the safe side, *my* side, of the field.

MY NEIGHBOR DARLA was ten and sat in the front of the white-kid bus as its monitor. She had views on the integration of our school and busing that bordered, according to many a political elementary schooler, on the communist. Her dad was a public defender, had gone through all kinds of fancy college in Chapel Hill. She believed like my mother (but I never would have voiced this on the bus) that black people were every bit as good and smart and deep-down decent and capable as white people (paternalistic language, language from the vantage point of relative privilege, sure, but *progressive* in its day). A person's skin color had no bearing on the quality of that person's character, she liked to say, parroting, no doubt, her hippie, pinko dad, who wouldn't even let her watch TV. She believed that black girls could be pretty, even though their facial features and hair weren't exactly—her word—"normal." She believed—and this was the kicker to many neighborhood kids listening while jostling along on their way to school—that every pool should be open to white people and black people, like the ones on all the

Hampton Roads military bases and housing complexes. In heated arguments with Jerry, the eleven-year-old genocide-promoting racist, she would concede on one point. In her equality crusade she promoted mixed swimming (there was chlorine) and schooling (there were remedial classes) and shopping (there was already a black mall and the newer, more suburban white mall) and dining (a scientific fact, she said, that black and white people have very different taste buds and will separate naturally). But she drew the line at water fountains. She said it like this: black people deserve equal rights in America, of course—of course!—but she wasn't going to drink after one.

ONE SATURDAY I GO to the new Sears superstore with my mom and dad. Who knows why? That's lost in the sinkhole of memory. But my parents were hard workers. They were house-proud and yard-proud. They believed the grass and flower beds and shrubs should look clean and sharp and good, just as they believed their boys should look clean and sharp and good. When you are a hopeful working-class American, when you are not so far from poor (in paychecks and genealogy), you carry yourself with outward signs of dignity and properness so no one mistakes you for lesser than how you wish yourself to be.

Maybe my father needed a rake, a sprinkler, some mulch.

The Sears is big like a warehouse, like an airplane hangar, a "box store" before that phrase is commonly used. I love coming here. I can walk by myself over to the toy section, then wander toward sporting goods—the bicycles and weights and golf clubs and basketballs. There is a lot of crime in Hampton in the 1970s, a lot of violence. (Every boy must be able to fight. How many fights have I seen by the time I'm seven? Ten, twelve? Split eyebrows. Popped noses. Ears red like paint. A tuft of after-battle ripped-out hair like a piece of abandoned bird's nest scuttling the sidewalk in a breeze.) But the mental image of the world, for my family at any rate, has not become a dangerous place yet, a place where one minute of TV violence or crime conveys the feeling of a thousand crimes right outside our door, right inside our heads. It's a television decade—the years of Manson with a swastika on his forehead and Squeaky Fromme giving interviews and handsome, smiling Ted Bundy and the Zodiac Killer and Son of Sam, and these are distinctly American characters delivering distinctly American chaos and sex and murder and apocalypse and their stories come filtered through and shot out of a box into our small living room and yet I roam through neighborhoods and stores and fields and parking lots. My life is an unpredictable adventure, often—at least in these memories—parent-free.

I know there is a pool table in the sporting goods section. Polished wood, green velvet. It's a display model. Anyone can play. A sign on the side says "Try Me." I turn a corner and see several black teenage boys, thirteen or fourteen years old, are playing. They are laughing, mocking one another for missed shots. I can't get to the bikes and punching bags without walking through them. So I stand at the end of an aisle, ten feet from the boys, and watch and wait. I think that when the boy shooting has to walk around the table for the next shot on the other side, I will squeeze by, keep my head down, be on my way.

What's up, little man? a smiling boy says, but seemingly to no one in particular because he's still looking at the lay of the balls on the table. He has on a Washington Redskins jersey. As I've been watching from a distance, he's been talking the whole time. All the other boys laugh at what he says. In fact, when he did a white country boy voice a few seconds ago—making fun, I think, of one of the white clerks who has been walking around, watching the boys—I smiled. He is kind of like a comedian on TV. (At seven I secretly think black people are funnier than white people because of shows like *What's Happening!!* and *Good Times* and *Sanford and Son*— Redd Foxx is a cranky genius, and that bit about the heart attack and how he looks to heaven and says "Elizabeth," oh man—even though many of the grownups I know are more like Archie Bunker in *All in the Family*, but somber, with no laugh track or opening or ending credits. And am I supposed to be with Archie or against him when he says words like "coon" and "faggot" and treats his wife like a maid? All this subtext and multivalence confuses me.)

The funny boy stands up after a shot and turns and looks directly at me. He says, *I said what's up, little man?*

I freeze.

This ain't our table, man, he says. *You can play if you want.*

He holds out the stick. What can I do? I take a step forward. There is only one thing I can do and that is what he is suggesting I do. I take the stick and don't think and walk over and lean over the table with the pool stick awkward in both hands and take a shot. I miss the white ball completely and leave a blue chalk streak on the table. The black kids laugh, but it's not mean, doesn't feel mean. Now *I* am the comedian. I keep trying to make a shot.

Oh, man, they say, giggling. *Oh man*, they say, out of breath from laughing as I miss a sixth and seventh and eighth time, leaving marks all over the table, some almost like gouges in the green. The boys are nearly falling down with laughter. *Oh, man.*

I'm seven, a little shy, but I like being the center of attention sometimes. So I'm not someone destroying property (that idea doesn't enter my mind). I'm an entertainer with some new and different friends—black friends, like that one black friend I had a couple years ago who couldn't come to my birthday and I couldn't go to his, Barry Fox—like Redd Foxx! This is like a scene on a black comedy show on TV, because white people appear in those shows—as racist devils (like landlords) or properly enlightened saviors (like teachers or anti-war liberals)—but black people rarely appear on white shows, almost never as serious actors in dramas, unless they are cop dramas in need of criminals or Mr. Jefferson moving into Archie Bunker's neighborhood to better display and focus and expose Archie's racism to raise the consciousness of the white audience, the real advertised-to demographic, at least a little bit.

Alright, the boy in the Redskins jersey says. *Alright. Little man, little man . . . let me show you how to do it.*

The other boys are still laughing, looking at the now-scuffed and nearly ruined table.

Redskins jersey says, *Like this here. You place this hand flat on the table near the white ball, then you lay the stick across your hand, right in this little groove here between your first finger and thumb. Then you line up the tip with the ball and try to slide your back arm like this here and hit the white ball hard right in the center with the tip. You don't wanna mess up the felt, little man, unless you're going to buy this table here.*

He is a good teacher. I think I understand.

He stands up straight, my new friend, and faces me and holds out the stick again to let me try to do it the right way.

Hey! a tall, thin white man shouts. He has on a navy polo shirt with "Sears" above the breast pocket. He is jogging toward us.

The boy in the Redskins jersey drops the stick onto the hard, white floor and it *clack clack clacks*. I stand there, paralyzed, as the black boys go sprinting through the department store, toward the outside doors, even though they didn't do anything but play pool on a table that they were invited, by a sign, to play on. The white man follows them but he is no match for their youth and speed.

I don't move for what seems like a long time but is probably only a minute or two.

My mother and father saw the boys running, wondered and worried about me, where I was, why those boys were running, what was going on. They are beside me now. *What happened?* they ask. *What happened? Why are those boys running? Did they do something? Did they take something? Did they bother you?*

After a long pause, thinking, I say, *They didn't bother me. They didn't take anything.*

The tall, thin white man walks back to the table, panting. He rasps like a smoker. He looks at the green velvet, scuffed and marked, and says, *That's it, those kids, those kids, they come in here and they aren't going to buy anything and then they ruin a nice pool table worth hundreds of dollars!* He keeps saying that now the table is worthless, unsellable. *This is ruined! Useless! No one will buy it! Useless!*

Who did this? my mother and father ask. *Did you see?*

Guilt is like gravity, holding me in place. I am only a kid. Still, I could be like a white savior on a black TV show made by white people (probably produced by Norman Lear at CBS and maybe criticized by Stokely Carmichael and Huey Newton of the Black

Panthers for its patronizing white gaze and its unflattering depictions of black poverty and family dysfunction, but I haven't heard of any of them yet); I could prove that there is justice in the world and people are people and don't jump to conclusions based on appearances and so on. I *could* do that. And this is a story and I could change the ending and make my younger self look better, a precocious social justice go-getter, a curious little not-racist white boy in a country and a region and a state built out of racism. But that's not what I do, what I did, not how I remember it, not who I was. I shrugged my shoulders. My face probably blushed. I wasn't going to sacrifice myself for some black kids I didn't know who'd already made their escape. I was learning how to *be* in this world—what to express and how, what to withhold. I said, *I didn't see anything. I heard the boys and walked over here and saw the table and then the boys took off running.* All true, just not the truth.

Life was a series of little survivals. I told a story to my parents and the Sears worker, and since this is America it was conveniently the one everyone already believed anyway.

MY DEAD GRANDFATHER, my father's father, owned a corner store—a "general store"—in Phoebus, a section of Hampton that is poor and all-black now (in 1979) but was not *as* poor and *as* all-black when he owned the store in the late 1950s and early '60s. History came sweeping into the neighborhood like mustard gas. But how? From where? What *is* history? Why does it feel like time and all the world's happenings funneled into a force haunting the present? Why do I feel, writing this sentence, remembering and reimagining myself as a child, like I have an illness called "history"?

I've collected information on the topic of the store—snippets, comments, references, words floating in the air (which is what words do, I think, before they disappear)—and I try to understand what happened.

It's the day after my ninth birthday, November 19, 1979. My grandmother is cooking (in my memory she is often cooking) and talking across the kitchen to other grown-ups—an uncle, an aunt, an older cousin. I watch. I listen.

The Iranians, in something the TV calls the Hostage Crisis (which has a different bright font and foreboding music on each of the three broadcast television networks for the evening news), have just released some women and all the black people—thirteen total— because women and especially black people have been oppressed by the ruling class of American whites. Black people and women should be in solidarity with Iranians against white American colonizers and, according to the revolutionaries in Iran, America's corrupt puppet, Iran's overthrown Shah, Mohammad Reza Pahlavi (whom the young Dick Cheney wanted to arm with nuclear weapons to fend off threats from Iraq, but I won't know that for decades). In this scenario—can this be right?—I am part of the ruling class, a colonizer, an oppressor. Sitting in this dilapidated kitchen.

My grandmother is talking about Iran, or rather she is talking about what she has gleaned about Iran from one- and two-minute snippets of TV news. She dropped out of school as an early teen (not uncommon in eastern North Carolina in the 1930s). Like me, she could not find Iran or even the Middle East on a map. She likes football, especially the Redskins, and soap operas and professional wrestling and the local and national news. The ladies she works with at the school cafeteria, hair-netted and plastic-gloved, often start a morning conversation during prep time where Walter Cronkite left off the night before.

She is mid-story now, so I pay attention. She is saying something about Iran and something about black people and something about white people not being oppressors and something about my dead grandfather's store. Everything is connected. History and the personal, my neighborhood and global events, overlap and tangle. And it is a shame that words disappear in the air. Otherwise I could work with them like puzzle pieces—moving them around, flipping them on their sides—to try to understand the world, how white people and black people and dictators and revolutionaries in Iran are connected.

When my dead grandfather owned the store, she is saying, it was the black people who were the oppressors, who were the downfall of it and of my grandfather. He opened it. He stocked it on credit. People came by and bought canned foods and cigarettes and beer and candy. He did all right. He struggled. Then it all went down because of them. Her face is angry and perplexed.

I follow the gist. I've heard versions before. My grandfather owned a place and worked hard to keep the place and help the people in the community. In my grandmother's telling, it was fine. For a while. There were no problems. But since I know the end of the story—a lost business, depression, health problems, money problems, an early death—I know that something tragic must have happened. Something inside of him that seems to have been caused by something outside of him.

In this part of my grandmother's story, the poor black people are responsible. They started moving into the neighborhood. But they'd go down a couple streets to the black-owned stores to buy their groceries. They didn't want to buy from my grandfather, she says. But I know, because of other conversations I've heard while with my father, that maybe my grandfather didn't want black people overtaking his store because they'd run off the whites, the ones left in the neighborhood, the ones who had more money to buy goods. So now, here in the small kitchen, I am starting to understand that my father and grandmother, a son and his mother, tell the same story, with the same basic facts, in very different ways. You can make events that happened mean different things—a word game!

To my father it was foolish of his father not to want to sell groceries to anybody, of any color. Money is money, he likes to say. It's all green.

To my grandmother, it was the black people who didn't want to buy groceries from my grandfather's store, through no fault of his.

In one version, my grandfather acts toward black people in a way that makes them know they are not wanted, that his is a white store.

In another version, my grandmother's this morning and at other times in the past, my grandfather is the victim of their boycott of his store, their racist and oppressive boycott, for no other reason than he is white. The black people are prejudiced against *him*, not the other way around. *They always say whites are prejudiced*, she says. *But it goes both ways, oh yes*, she says. *I'm living proof. I'd like a handout*, she says. *Where's my handout? Where's my government check? Where's my almost-free housing? What about helping the struggling* white *people, the* Americans?

My father has told me to always listen to my grandmother when she talks because that is the polite thing to do. Respect your elders. So of course that is what I do: sit in the kitchen and let story fill the air around me and don't interrupt. Thing is, my father also told me that some of her stories are twisted in a way to make the world fit more comfortably inside of her idea of it.

Sitting here listening, thinking about Iran and black people and my grandfather's store, I believe that if a person could control all the stories he could control the whole world. That would be the greatest super power, something not even Superman or murderous Pol Pot (whom I also heard about on TV) could do.

In the car, on the way home, my father says that my grandmother has a "funny" memory sometimes. He says she keeps the parts of stories she likes and builds them up. Then she cuts the parts of stories she doesn't like. Otherwise she'd get too sad. He looks at me in the passenger seat. Sunlight fills the car. We drive out of the memory, into the future. Otherwise I'd get too sad.

First Car, 1978

AND THERE IS THE STORY of my father's first car, the car before the Mustang (awesome and shining fire-engine red in the driveway), the car my father bought all by himself when he was in high school. He worked at his father's store, cut neighbors' grass, stacked wood, anything. He saved and he saved and then bought an old—what? Ford? Chevy? I don't know. Details are scarce. I'm eight, nine maybe. I've pieced this story together from a thousand half stories, anecdotes, mere sentences, phrases, all spread out over years. (So much of how we come to know things is exactly like this: dubiously, imperfectly.)

Deprivation kills a person (quickly or slowly) or breeds resourcefulness, common sense, and focus. Instability as the basic reality of a life can lead a person, a driven person, on a journey toward a more controlled, defined existence, predictability. One seeks what one lacks. It's Darwinian. My father embodied that—

cleverness, work, work, work. Don't stop to think too much. Don't be soft. Just do.

The story of the car is the story of my father and his father. It is, in a way, the story of me, too, because while we are more than our past, we are always part past, but I don't know this as a boy.

It goes something like this: My grandfather wrecked his own car, or it was in the shop—details change depending on who's doing the telling. My grandfather borrowed my father's car. This was when the general store was struggling, money was drying up—pressure from outside, confusion inside, chaos in his thoughts, no way out. The world was changing—the world was out of his control. Being white in the South was easier than being black in the South, sure, but assumptions were so different for white people like my grandfather and black people. Whites were part of a mythologized story of rising and redemption and promise—America was my grandfather's country, right? Every political story, including the Westerns he loved, told him so. The newspaper said as much. Every TV show said as much. *See? That's him on TV, the silent hero!* He should be rising, on top of the world. Black people—well, my grandfather didn't worry about black people until all this civil rights nonsense, until they encroached (so he believed) on his life, like not buying from his store because *they* were racist. My grandfather was depressed by the mess of his life juxtaposed against the commonplace expectations for whites in a country of supposed opportunity. He dreamed the way he was taught to dream and the dream turned out to be a lie. Who was responsible? Whose lie? If history was hard to understand, what about belief, faith, a shifting sense of your own reality?

And he didn't have a car. And my father—at seventeen or eighteen—did. So my grandfather borrowed my father's car, which my father loved, and he drove that car, despondent, off of a bridge and into the James River.

Amazing, no, the end of that last sentence? Yet absolutely true.

A sailor from Norfolk jumped off the bridge and into the James and saved my grandfather. It was in the papers. Once my father knew his father would survive, it became yet another embarrassment, another lost or destroyed thing. My grandfather was injured (I don't know the specifics). He was in the hospital for a few days. My father dropped out of high school to run the store (he later went back to school and struggled to finish at twenty years old).

So what do working-class and poor black people and white people in the South have in common besides DNA and God? I'll tell you: angina, heart disease, hypertension, diabetes, sleepless nights, worry, hope, a risk for stroke, love, more worry, money problems, love, stress, bills, kids, joy, parents, siblings, stepsiblings, half-siblings, cousins by the dozen, spouses, ex-spouses, phone calls they want to avoid, someone close to them with addiction problems, dreams, pain, depression, anxiety, more love, more hope, futures that scare them, and too often, broken fucking hearts.

One day I asked my mom how my grandfather, long dead from a heart attack by then, managed to drive Dad's first car off of a bridge. She hesitated. Then she said maybe he fell asleep because he couldn't remember anything in the hospital.

Later, on some other day, I asked my father. He looked at me. He asked how I knew about that, what I knew about that. I said I'd just heard people, relatives, tell different parts of the story. After a while I put it together: My grandfather drove my young father's first car off a bridge into a big, brackish Virginia river and then a sailor jumped into the water and saved him and was a hero and it was all in the newspaper. If there was any consolation, in fact, any mild reduction in my father's sense of shame, it was that the article focused more on the glowing heroism of the sailor—very much like a hero on TV—and less on the despairing, unlucky life of the driver.

I didn't think my father would answer my question that day. Then, after thinking about it, thinking about how to say the truth—some part or version of the truth—to a child, he said his father was not very good at paying attention sometimes. He said his father, my grandfather, whom I never knew, was a little lost late in his life and prone to confusion and accident.

HE LUMBERED AROUND a friend's neighborhood on the other side of the city, slow and friendly, a 250-pound innocent searching yard to yard for a companion. His name was Calvin. He was black, his dad was some kind of middle manager for a trucking company, he lived in one of the better blocks of the nicer nearby black neighborhoods, and he was almost always out playing with young white boys. My friends from this strange neighborhood—a more solidly middle-class place, higher levels of education, professional-class folks, slightly less anxious about school—said he "talked white" and that's why he didn't have any black friends (the black kids called him an Oreo, an Uncle Tom). My friends said he was "different," not "like them," and "OK." And no one had any problem that summer with the fact that he was ten years older than the kids with whom he played, and I think it goes without saying that we would not have known, especially in the context of ongoing racial tensions, how to have a relationship with a black person we saw as fully our equal or clearly superior to us by kid standards—video games, sports, your-momma jokes.

(Is my memory this wrong, or were the mid- to late 1970s in urban/ suburban Virginia so different in their awareness and vigilance around situations we'd immediately view as potentially predatory now? No, I think it was that parents were not involved in the daily activities of their children, that alarmist media hadn't infiltrated every curve of the human brain, that I roamed sidewalks and fields and backyards and parks like a cautious animal sniffing new territory. Neighborhoods were everything, enclaves of kid interest, boredom, and ideas. Adults were busy. Kids were free.)

Hey, y'all, Calvin would say. *Hey, y'all.* Then he'd walk over to wherever my friends and I were playing. He was usually wearing the same gray sweatpants and black and gray horizontally striped shirt. He had little bits of leaves in his hair—from where was a mystery, but probably from wooded shortcuts. Around his mouth was always a faint ghost of morning toothpaste. Some kids called him a *total freakin' retard* behind his back (though his sister was evidently famous as some kind of

super-straight-A-spelling-bee-winning brainiac), but when he showed up he was welcomed. He'd be It the whole game of tag in the woods, no complaints. He was the best blocker in football, crashing through bony, white ten-year-olds as if they were so much brittle brush, flinging kids to the ground where they left matted grass, dents in the soft earth, before they jumped up for the next snap.

That year—what year?—1979? '80?—anyway, that year, some year—we all went to 7-Eleven to play the new pinball game. Little kid heroin: every quarter we could scrounge went into that machine.

But there was a system, a protocol, a culture around the game. Kids had to know it. You put a quarter on the game, leaning on a little ledge in the corner above the bumper buttons. That meant you had next game. Quarter next to yours, on the left, had game after that, etc. *Got next*, we'd say, and everyone knew what that meant. *Next. Next. Got next.*

One day, not paying attention, one of my friends, a kid named Steve, put a quarter into the machine and started playing, even though there was a quarter *on the ledge* already, holding next game. Kid named Mikey comes over, says, *What the hell, man? What the . . . ?* He's big. He's tough. Older brothers. Drunk, abusive dad. He's like the neighborhood ass kicker. He yanks Steve's shirt, throws him on the ground, and finishes his game. Then he tells me and Steve and a couple other kids that we can't play anymore pinball today. He'll be keeping any quarters left on the machine. Thanks.

Next time Calvin comes around, Steve says, *Hey, Calvin, man, you won't believe this, but, man, Mikey was at the 7-Eleven calling you a, you know, the N-word. Said it like five times. Calvin's a blank. Calvin's a you-know-what. Said it over and over.*

Now my friend's neighborhood buddies and Calvin and I don't know that blackness, as I am now discussing it, as it is defined by white people at this moment in time, is an American thing, an ideological, sociopolitical construct, a set of assumptions and value judgments based on economic and cultural history and dominant white power structures stretching back hundreds of years and kept in place with violence and death and treaties and laws. Hell no, we don't know that. Don't know much really—I'm like, what, nine and three-quarters and a week? I just exist. We spend more time pondering the varying consistencies of our boogers than we do thinking about why Calvin's skin seems to mean one thing and ours another. And Calvin isn't going to help us here. What he does know, even though he has learning issues, is that the N-word is like a rope, a pack of dogs, a water cannon. He doesn't need to know history to feel its weight. No one does. One day when he was a little kid, his biggest problem was that his bookish sister ate all the good cereal; next day, *bam*, some crazy information, a mysterious self-consciousness, got all up inside his head and he was black. He was a *big black guy* that some people were afraid of. He plays football and tag with a bunch of much younger white boys because he believes we are his friends (we are, in a way) and would never think a word like that about him.

For weeks after Steve lied to Calvin, my friends and I owned the pinball machine because word got around that Calvin was looking for Mikey and his friends, that he'd be waiting outside the 7-Eleven every day until they were man enough to show up and call him the N-word to his face.

Every so often Steve would walk outside and talk to Calvin. *Seen 'em, Calvin? Any sign yet, Calvin? Gotta show up sometime, Calvin.*

Then Steve would come back in to play pinball with my friends and me.

I remember this because one day Steve, who was getting ready to turn eleven, who I imagine grew up to be a successful professional and maybe a baseball coach and an active member of the community (school board parent? city council?), walked back into the store, pointed at Calvin waiting outside in the blistering heat, and joked, *Hey, guys, hey, guys, maybe this is what it felt like to have a slave.*

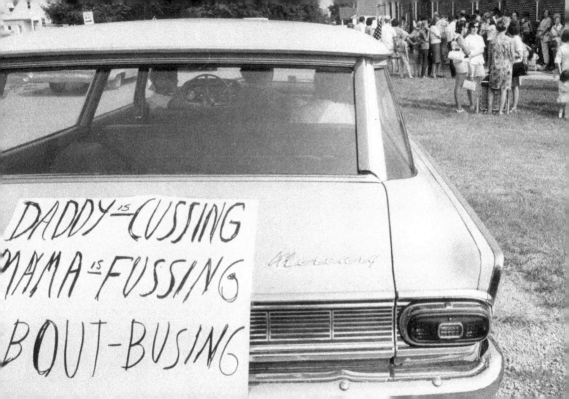

ONE DAY WHEN I AM SIX a sense of shame about my family parks in my mind and forms a lump in my throat and I ask my mom if she can stop driving the bus for the poor black kids. On the playground, in the fields, climbing trees in the woods, some kids keep saying my mom is the "zoo keeper," that my family may as well be black. *Go live in Pine Chapel!* kids joke. *Ghetto Greg! Hahahahahaha!* My mom is, according to some kids, the world's biggest N-word lover.

It's dawn. My father is off to work (in my memory, which is sometimes like a snippet of running film when it is not like some other metaphor, he is leaving or coming home, and the massive space and expanse of time where he is *not located in my experience* is a mysterious condition called "work"). Mom sits with me at the breakfast table. I eat Rice Krispies.

She doesn't answer my question. Instead she tells me that when she was a teenager, in the early 1960s, she and her friends, in calf-length dresses and Spalding shoes and bobby socks, spent afternoons at the pharmacy in town, where they had a soda fountain: a simple white counter with six metal, swivel stools, each stool with an orange, faux-leather seat, all bolted to the floor. The girls would order sodas and floats and shakes, turn this way and that on the stools, talk about . . . girl things, she says.

She says our country is big. Our country is changing. Black people walk into white bathrooms, but they couldn't not very long ago. They drink from water fountains, sit up front on public buses, but they couldn't not very long ago. They can go to any restaurant and expect to be served, just like us. Some white people—people like us—don't like these changes, don't know why anything needs to change at all. And because we are a big country, she says, with a lot of different kinds of people and different people want different things . . . Or, she pauses, thinks . . . Some people, well, they get afraid of big, big changes in such a big, big country. And some very bad things have happened because people who are afraid act out. They misbehave. Do I understand? Some people have hurt other people. Some people have even done worse things than that. She says she remembers her father, my papa, watched Walter Cronkite talk about all this on their new Zenith, which was her family's first TV. But she didn't think too much about these things when she was young because her world was just happy, the way she wants my world to be, just happy and safe, and her world was a girl's world and she had my dad, who wasn't my dad yet, and her friends and her family. She was never allowed near the black parts of town, especially the parts she drives a bus through now, so she didn't know any black people. None. The talk coming out of Papa's Zenith, the history of slavery, Jim Crow, the new Civil Rights Act President Kennedy addressed the nation about on June 11, 1963, five months before he was assassinated in Dallas—what was that to her? There were dances. Boys. Friends. Parties. Gossip. She was so lucky she says, because she got to have a good life and never had to think about it or worry about it being taken away.

But then one day, on the way home from somewhere, she went to the pharmacy to see if any of her friends were there. She saw that all the stools had been unbolted from the floor. The soda fountain had been closed. No more ice cream or root beer floats for anyone. She asked the owner, an old white man she had spoken to many times before, what happened. The owner, this quiet man, this polite man, this churchgoing man, this gentleman in most ways you could observe and name, understood it was the law now and he had to serve black teenagers as well as whites. He could get in trouble if he didn't, he said. He had decided to close the soda fountain, remove all the stools, and stick, as he had originally done, to drugs and remedies, soaps and lotions and hair products. The pharmacy was no longer a place to gather. A "No Loitering" sign appeared. It wasn't about the black kids, the owner said. He'd been meaning to do this, he said, to simplify things.

What do you think about that story? she asks.

I concentrate, finishing my Rice Krispies. *Well*, I say, *no one could get ice cream.*

That's right, she says. *But why?*

She is a storyteller. A Christian. A Methodist who believes that a person's truth is in their deeds. A child gets how stories work, how they contain clues to their deeper meanings. So I know the answer: *Because people are afraid*, I say.

That's right, she says. *But we aren't afraid, are we?*

I say no, but I'm not sure that's true.

Then she says, *Would you think it was fair if someone said you couldn't have ice cream because of the way you look?*

That makes no sense at all: *NO!*

I don't think that would be fair either, she says. Then she smiles, rubs her hand through my hair, and says, *Now hurry up. We'll be late.*

PRESIDENT JOHNSON AGAIN: "If you can convince the lowest white man he's better than the best colored man, he won't notice you're picking his pocket. Hell, give him somebody to look down on, and he'll empty his pockets for you."

José Ortega y Gasset, the early twentieth-century Spanish philosopher and essayist, wrote one of the best and truest sentences I know: "I am I and my circumstance," sometimes translated to the more vernacular "I am I and what's around me." A powerful strain in our national character pulls in the exact opposite direction from this sentiment. Something like "I am I. Now get off my property." As a boy, I learned *not* to see that I lived immersed in the reverberations of American slavery, walked down streets named after Native American chiefs, and went to a school the local government named after a general on the losing side of an insurrectionist war.

American mythologies—and much American Christian mythology especially, my childhood world—exalts the individual, the singular person who arose fully formed in the image of the maker. More mechanistic views of human ecology, of interconnected systems and history—that invisible social forces shape us, steer life and thought without our seeing or understanding—are not a natural fit in the American and Southern psyche. In fact, our confrontation with these views can cause a painful shattering of delusions, instigating a kind of truth and reconciliation inside the self. Or, conversely, they can bring forth incensed denials and self-justifications. I think of the common Southern phrase I heard throughout my childhood: "hogwash."

For instance, an educated, liberal white mind—let's take that as our subject (and I mean the aware citizen in a small *l* liberal democracy based on civic governance and freedoms and laws for all, not left politics)—can lean on an accepted theory of American urban black poverty, one crystalline example of the "race problem," in places like Hampton and Newport News (the basketball star Allen Iverson called it "Newport Bad News"): there has obviously been a history of inequality and profoundly unjust social systems. This has obviously cordoned off the poor and those outside of power, through housing and education and judicial policies, through court actions and laws and attitudes, in legalese and spasms of brutality, over decades and centuries. This obvious American reality—with a clear line back to the Atlantic slave trade, chattel slavery, Jim Crow, policies like Massive Resistance in Virginia, realities like school-to-prison pipelines operational all over the country right now—has caused an unceasing set of negative and generationally compounding pressures on lives, families, and communities. These pressures are traumatic and continuous, creating despair and hopelessness, desperation. When communities physically and socially break down, they can morally break down. Chaos is a by-product. Innocent lives are born into overwhelming impediments. The cycle repeats. The educated, liberal mind says: That is a problem! Not *my* problem, but certainly a problem! We must really figure out how to fix it! Some college courses would be good!

The tougher part, I think, the less obvious part outside of corners of the academic social sciences and humanities, is to acknowledge whiteness as the most powerful force in all this, the original frame, the political fuel running the engine, creating the movements and configurations, and to start to see, in a commonsense way, American and Southern history from 30,000 feet above, as the expression goes. Then we see the "ghetto" and the all-white, affluent, gated community are extreme economic and social outcomes of the same history, the same policies, laws, actions, and cultural stories. (Sure, people—rich and poor and in between, white and black and other—succeed and fail in innumerable ways within this racialized system, absolutely, but it is a lot easier to *not notice this system* when you aren't getting punished by it because of something as strange as skin pigmentation.

And the truths borne out in data [the CDC lists the "premature death" rate as 50 percent higher for black Americans than white Americans] are not supplanted by any anecdotal personal experiences, regardless of how often these are used to counter statistics.)

White people I know often don't want to hear this history stuff. I get that. I do. A policy like affirmative action can seem unfair to some unless you do this tougher-part, wider-view *history* thing and see that affirmative action, of a kind, has been roaring for more than 240 years in America. Then you see affirmative action, as it exists now, as akin to blowing on a giant lake as a way to change its temperature.

It is easier to turn from these ideas, to run back into those American, libertarian notions about the autonomous individual, the singular life only connected to the past and other lives as it sees fit, as it finds acceptable, or to on some conscious or unconscious level believe in the most pernicious racist myth of all, a staple of the far right and so-called "alt-right," the younger, more tech-savvy collection of white, male supremacists terrorizing a message board, comments section, or social media platform near you: that black people—that all people without Caucasian skin and features—are not "real" Americans, when in fact Europeans and Africans arrived on what became Virginia shores (where Native Americans lived) at roughly the same time—one as colonists, in 1607, the other as tools and property, in 1619.

English novelist D. H. Lawrence, in *Studies in Classic American Literature*, published in 1923, only sixty years after Lincoln's Emancipation Proclamation, wrote of the curious belief in an "essential white America," which he saw, as he traveled and briefly lived in Mexico and the U.S. Southwest, as a limited and convenient national origin story, editing out and deleting almost everything else, especially Native Americans and Hispanics. He marveled at the psychological power of this race narrative, the religious zeal of it.

Maybe the key to progress in a broader understanding of the weapon and the wound of systematic racism (as opposed to one's personal views) in America and the South is to learn to present the origins and elements of white racial identity—the macro-level issue—without the finger-pointing at individuals, because I know my grandparents and great-grandparents were circumscribed by their class and the needs of their unrelenting present circumstances and felt pride and protectiveness and pain about who they were, where they were born, and to whom. They were provincial not by choice, of course, but by the organizing forces of their lives. They were not *anti*-intellectual; they existed outside the intellectual, untouched by the social and cultural privilege I enjoy, in a different set of facts and subjective realities. To confront them with accusation and indictment would have ended any conversation a few words in. If I told them that racism in our area was not a black problem but a white force, damaging black people and, over time, deranging and corrupting white people, they might have made an emergency call to the doctor or the minister.

The abstractions of history and language and theory—the clouds in which I daydream—almost never find purchase in resource-scarce living situations, an embodied knowledge of which can make the academic genealogically of the lower and working socioeconomic classes—me again—walk through ivory-tower halls with a chip on his shoulder roughly the size and weight of one of those IBM computer monitors from the 1980s. Some days I feel like a lost tourist, staring across a smoke-filled field of warring American meanings.

Maybe there is a way to raise consciousness about race, neutralize antagonisms, and reduce fear somewhat, somehow, among resistant whites. To make common knowledge how individuals exist in complex networks of social and cultural connection. To find better, more effective ways to describe racial valuing in the public square and in policies and practices as a vexing American phenomenon and a moral issue that has played out over time and into the present moment in all aspects of life, learning, and knowing. To be more logical than emotional and to show how inherent political empowerment or disempowerment related to skin color has no basis in science, rationality, and fact. To show equality and opportunity are in no way zero-sum. To bend emotion (the electric charge many white people feel when faced with the myriad instances and aspects of their possible complicity in structural racism) toward realities rather than further obfuscations. I don't know. I don't have the answers. I'm still trying to formulate the right questions, to think of what stories might be most useful to tell.

I lucked into having a very good mother, a person for whom kindness is a bottom line. She choked up telling me the stories I use in this book about her memory of the stark isolation of the first black student, Robert Rice Jr., at Hampton High School in 1961 and those stools removed from a pharmacy during the time of national sit-ins.

She's still a Methodist, and she's a Southerner through and through. I think you could call her a progressive Christian—a multicultural, multiracial, multiethnic constituency spread across the country and increasingly more interested in better understanding and promoting social justice issues and reform; they just haven't historically shouted and waved signs and cast aspersions and worried aloud about other people's human and constitutional rights to get noticed (though she has recently, in her mid-seventies, marched and waved signs for social justice causes).

My mother has always "lived the gospel"—volunteering, helping out needy families of all races and ethnicities, working with the disabled. Her life and attitudes remind me—and she has never pondered early critical race theory in legal studies, or anti-racist philosophy, or a structuralist reading of Southern history—that below all the noise and confusion of culture, decency is still a more natural state than indecency. Indecency is a corruption built on fear, a veneration of ignorance, and selfishness. Indecency is in every way anti-Gospel, anti-Jesus, anti-Christian.

She believes the Golden Rule works all the time and in every situation, big and small. She encouraged me to imagine. Imagine you are a black rather than white child. Imagine you look out the window of the bus in Hampton in 1975 and that the world out there doesn't want you, the world fears you and seemingly hates you for no reason you can understand. Imagine you are that black rather than white child and grow up and walk through public spaces and have sparks of suspicion follow you, and those sparks of suspicion make your very existence precarious. Imagine what that might do to you over time. Imagine how that would feel. Imagine—just imagine—if you were that black rather than white child and some white people, because of the stupid luck of history, didn't, couldn't, believe in the complexity and richness of your interior life, your thinking and connecting and creating and communicating, your heart, your soul.

I can carry this imagination, these thought experiments, further, of course, toward examples that should be more obvious than they apparently are. Imagine George Zimmerman gunning down a suburban white kid (or even a poor and troubled white kid) in a hoodie and how well Florida's "stand your ground" law would have held up in court and conservative media. Imagine a white Walter Scott getting shot five times from behind while loping away in fear for his life by North Charleston police officer Michael Slager, which was caught on video, and having a South Carolina state jury, in a first trial, deadlock on murder charges and result in a mistrial. Imagine the response to three hundred young black men with torches and shouting menacing chants as they marched through the grounds of the University of Virginia, where I went to graduate school. Imagine mixed-race Barack Obama—Kansas kid by way of Hawaii, white mom and conservative white grandparents, Harvard Law grad, constitutional law professor—trying to get elected with Donald Trump's six bankruptcies, three marriages, a penchant for paranoid conspiracy, a history of philandering, bragging about sexual predation and assault on tape, celebrating meanness and cruelty on social media, and telling easily verifiable lies with regularity. Pull up YouTube and take a look at the Funny or Die sketch "The Black NRA," one of the most useful and accessible and darkly funny examples of semiotic theory in action, as well as a presentation of America's racialized meanings and the bleak contextual and contingent nature of hot national emotion and belief.

But I should keep these thought experiments scaled down, personal. I imagine my father was black instead of white. Does he get the loan to buy the small, brick house I lived in as a boy? Does he get offered, in the 1970s and without a college degree, an opportunity to work at the Newport News shipyard with computers, which were data and information storage devices and organizers that filled up entire large rooms? Does he sell the small house in a "good" (read: white) neighborhood in Hampton and use the profit to buy a bigger, better house in the suburbs, as part of the mass migration of white flight away from urban areas in the late 1970s and '80s? Do I get to go to that "good school" (read: white) with a college prep curriculum in the suburbs as a teenager? Does he get to use the acquisition of wealth from property and employment advancement to increase his credit, to invest, to help me be the first in my family to go to college? Do I get to be a professor, with whatever capital and status that implies, and write this book? At what point in this chain of events would racism have stopped his opportunities, and thus stopped mine? And of course what about stepping back another generation and pondering his father and mother, or their fathers and mothers? How many opportunities, or even lives, disappear as we move backward through civil rights, Jim Crow, Reconstruction, the Civil War, slavery? This one Southern American past, in North Carolina and Virginia, is different with darker skin, the future of this past rewritten. I think I likely disappear. Extrapolate from there.

I know from experience that notions of complex structural racism and white supremacy (this latter as social phenomenon, not uncle so-and-so's offensive comments at the cookout) are encountered by many in America the way Europeans and Americans probably engaged with the new knowledge of germs and bacteria as causes of disease and disease transmission in the 1860s, when Louis Pasteur made public his discoveries. This is all so abstract, so invisible to the naked eye, so beyond individual experience and easy comprehension. For a long time after Pasteur's discoveries, many Europeans and Americans continued to view disease as caused by spirits, or punishment for bad deeds, or lack of faith, or just bad luck. In fact, as science made strides to better inform people and improve their health with basic education, many retreated into more comfortable superstition, unable or unwilling to face such a paradigm shift in their understanding of the world. Paradigm shifts can be painful and disorienting, recasting, reorganizing, and even obliterating the comfort of what was formerly known. We see a similar pattern in regard to structural racism and white supremacy. As huge swaths of an ever more multicultural America accept advancing understandings of American race and a history of carefully constructed and government-sanctioned inequality, we also see a frightening rise in white ethnonationalism in politics, viral race-based conspiracy theories on social media, and a normalization of more explicitly racist commentary in what are considered mainstream conservative radio and television outlets.

In 1951, after the devastation and mass murder of World War II, Hannah Arendt, in *The Origins of Totalitarianism*, wrote that the imperial mind, the precursor to totalitarian regimes, far-right fascist and far-left communist, begins with racism as a way to justify its increasingly immoral and anti-democratic deeds. She also wrote that "[t]he sad truth is that most evil is done by people who never make up their minds to be good or evil."

What I am saying for now is this: I lived among President Johnson's "lowest white man," was a kind of lowest white boy. I was cloaked every day in cultural and political stories. They were complicated and confusing and absurd. Of course I believed many of them. Why would a child doubt the prevailing stories around him?

What I am saying is this: it is easy and convenient in the babel of hyper-mass-mediated America for white citizens to be incurious about our actual history regarding institutionalized racism—easier and easier every day.

What I am saying is this: the real, insidious power of racism the world over, and in America and the South and my boyhood city in particular, is its ability, in human culture and thought and the nuances of communication, in individual and social psychology, to achieve normalcy in the minds of those benefitting and then take on the character of unquestioned truth.

The world, in human terms, has always been the set of stories we believe about the world.

Photograph Credits

Protest on Wheels, August 26, 1970. (Photograph by Don Pennell, P.71.37.07)

Anti-busing Rally, August 26, 1970. (Photograph by Don Pennell, P.71.37.04)

School Bus Stuck, September 1, 1970. (Photograph by Michael O'Neil, P.71.37.145)

Anti-busing Gathering, August 26, 1970. (Photograph by Don Pennell, P.71.37.05)

Happiness Is When Pools Open; They Were Open Yesterday at Chestnut Oaks, the Hamlet, Three Chopt, May 29, 1965. (V.66.10.43a)

Adults Usher Children to School Bus, September 21, 1970. (P.71.37.16)

Decorating Car before Anti-busing Motorcade, February 17, 1972. (P.74.11.18j)

Save Our Neighborhood Schools Rally, February 10, 1972. (P.74.11.18e)

At Massad's Restaurant, March 7, 1970. (P.71.01.41)

James Carlton Removing Rebel Flag from Car, February 18, 1972. (P.74.11.18i)

Singing Protest, May 5, 1968. (FIC.033206)

T. C. Boushall Middle School, September 2, 1986. (Photograph by Carl Lynn, V.91.04.231)

Anti-busing Speaker, February 9, 1972. (Photograph by Don Long, P.74.11.18d)

Anti-busing Protest, February 11, 1972. (P.74.11.18f)

Mobilizing for Busing Protest, February 10, 1972. (P.74.11.18o)

Wheelie Dealers, January 29, 1984. (V.85.37.4106)

Anti-busing Rally at the Capitol, August 29, 1970. (P.71.37.12)

Anti-busing Demonstration at State Republican Convention, June 27, 1970. (P.71.25.37)

Waiting for the Bus to School, August 31, 1970. (P.71.37.14)

In Protest, August 31, 1970. (P.71.37.13)

Students Gather at Monroe Park, May 5, 1968. (FIC.033205)

About the Author

GREG BOTTOMS is a professor of English at the University of Vermont. He is the author of several books, including *Angelhead: My Brother's Descent into Madness*, *The Colorful Apocalypse: Journeys in Outsider Art*, and *Spiritual American Trash: Portraits from the Margins of Art and Faith*.

CPSIA information can be obtained
at www.ICGtesting.com
Printed in the USA
BVHW020644200919
558972BV00002BA/4/P